TABLE OF CONTENT

INTRODUCTION...1

    Farinah 1

    Farux 1

    The Rites of Passage of Farinah 1

FOREWORD 2

Chapter 1 4

    •   The Child Within 4

Chapter 2 7

    •   The Woman Sage who was supposed to be a man 7

Chapter 3 13

    •   Life from a Cosmic Perspective..13

Chapter 4 17

    •   The Fountain of Youth 17

Chapter 5 20

    •   Is There A God? 20

Chapter 6 26

    What Love Has To Do With Marriage? 26

Chapter 7 30

    •   Who Is Sage Chioma?...30

Chapter 8 35

    •   What Is Death and After Life?..35

Chapter 9 40

- What Are Our Curable Secrets? 40

Chapter 10 46

- Who Is Sadiq and The Three Visitors? 46

Chapter 11 51

- Who Is A Mysticmorphosist™ 51

Chapter12 65

- What Is Cosmic Consciousness? 65

Chapter 13 67

- Awakening The Sage Within 67

    - Mystic Secret Key # 1 69

    - Mystic Secret Key # 2 73

    - Mystic Secret Key # 3 78

    - Mystic Secret Key # 4 81

    - Mystic Secret Key # 5 85

Closing Gathering...94

Sage Chioma...95

Mystic Tikimotu 95

Mystic Mokito 96

The Anointed One 96

Princess Sharon..102

Mystic Madiba 103

Library of Congress Cataloging • Publishing Data:
ISBN 978-0-9779716-3-3

INTRODUCTION

The Sage Within is a Journey of the Soul in search of answers to the ancient questions "From Whence We Came and Where Are We Going?"

It is a journey that we all would like to take on a daily basis, but due to manmade priorities, we find every reason why we cannot embark on such a spiritual journey.

Farinah lived 25 thousand feet above sea level in a village called Watanama where males are groomed to be Sages. They are taught how man and nature should live in harmony in order to have a balance between Mother Earth, energy and vibration.

Farux, the village chief Sage and the father of Farinah, is perplexed and confused by his seven year old daughter's inquisitiveness, understanding of the universe and her refusal to accept gender limitations. This is creating problems for the village, since only males are allowed to participate in spiritual ceremonies and studies.

The Rites of Passage of Farinah, the first female Sage, support the fact that energy and vibration has no gender, and is thus, available to all who want it. Let us take a journey into the world of energy and vibration by going back in time, so we can walk side-by-side with Farinah during her journey in search of The Sage Within.

Sharon Parris-Chambers
Negril, Jamaica, W.I.

1

FOREWORD

Theo Chambers in his new book "The Sage Within," shares his potentially life changing insights and beliefs on a wide range of very important human issues. In his first book, "God vs. Judaism & Christianity," he used the powerful Socratic teaching tool, the question, to invite the reader to find his/her own answers from within. In this work he calls on an equally effective instrument for instruction, the story.

And what a story! It's about a mythical woman-sage, Farinah, from an ancient land and her own indwelling knowledge that she freely shares with family and community. Through the skill of Theo's storytelling, Farinah's wisdom visits us and sheds a bright light on a wide array of critical and often perplexing issues – the true nature of reality, the chemistry of life, the potential of the child, the power and proper place of the woman in society, nutrition, health, prosperity, technology and on and on and on.

It is fascinating to experience how a single story can lead the reader down so many winding pathways in search of truth and clarity. Just as how a question is an invitation not just to find 'an answer' so this story's real goal is not so much about leading you to its destination, as it is about helping us to continue our own journey.

The Bible reminds us that if we ask, if we seek, if we knock we will receive, we will find and doors will open. I believe that this book is for the seeker, the asker and the one who knocks. It is intended for those who have a sincere desire to find.

To such a one I say 'read on' and as an important personality in the story, the Mystic Madiba promised - after climbing a great hill, one only finds that there are many more hills to climb.

Thank you Theo for selflessly baring your soul and sharing your light.

Dr. Tony Vendryes
Montego Bay, Jamaica

Chapter 1

Farinah was asked during one of her village mastermind gatherings, where did she learn so much about the Universe and Mother Nature and her answer was, "from the child within."

- ### *The Child Within*

"I recalled vividly that while I was in the womb of my earthly mother, I was able to listen to conversations the wise men of the village were debating, while my mother was busy preparing food for them," said Farinah.

My mother never heard one word of the wise men's conversation because women were not allowed in those meetings. While I was in the womb, I was not aware that I was a woman. I had no mental or spiritual limitations.

Being a free spirit, I was able to penetrate the walls of my mother's womb and sit among those wise elders and absorb their philosophies about who created the universe, and how we came to be here on Mother Earth.

I had no idea that one day I was going to leave the comfort of my earthly mother's womb and be physically among those elders I was communicating with through energy and vibration.

Farinah told the group; "I was able to communicate directly with Planets, Stars, Atoms and Earthly elements such as Air, Water, Earth, Sulfur, Mercury and Salt because energy and vibration have no walls or limitations."

Farinah explained: "life within the womb is like when you are waking up, but still between sleep and wakefulness. You are in a weightless state. You are aware of your surroundings, but totally unaware of the presence of your physical body."

"During one of my spiritual uninvited visits with the wise men of the village, they spoke about war and competition as if it was an earthly phenomenon.

Well, I must say that my first encounter with competition was feeling the force of thousands of male sperms trying to penetrate the egg that was responsible for my earthly manifestation.

I can still feel those forces within. I know the male sperm and female egg that are responsible for my temporary physical presence on this plane.

The group was amazed with Sage Farinah's recollection since her origin, especially when she said: "when the victorious sperm penetrated the egg, there was an explosion that triggered the universe within that egg, which activated the intelligence within.

Those activated intelligent cells were able to identify the female egg and male sperm genetic codes. Once the code of both the male and female were identified, those intelligent creators (gods) knew exactly what had to be done to create me, who now have the trace (DNA) of both my earthly mother's and father's codes."

Farinah decided that upon her departure from the comfort of the womb, she was not going to be involved in the human material world because it was going to force her energy and vibration to learn about subjects that she felt would directly interfere with her spiritual ability to communicate with the universe and her internal intelligent cells.

5

Farinah stated: "man's ignorance of the Universe is due to his creation of an active and rapid evolving material world that is not integrated or in harmony with the laws of energy and vibration." She further stated that: "Because of that, many have lost their innocent childhood gift to speak to bygone ancestors and to The Sage Within."

She concluded her explanation about the journey in search of The Sage Within by saying: "When earthly materialistic man comes to the clear understanding that the Atoms, Nitrogen, Carbon and Oxygen that comprise life on earth, are the same Atoms, Nitrogen, Carbon and Oxygen that were scattered across the universe when stars collapsed and spread their guts across the galaxy, then, we all can have a common understanding of the importance of us living in harmony with the Laws of Nature.

Farinah made a powerful point when she said: "When we look up to the sky, we should not only be aware that we are in the universe, but that the elements of the universe are within each of us."

Chapter 2

Sage Farinah's popularity spread like wildfire and she was invited to some of the most prestigious philosophical and spiritual gatherings of the time. One such invitation came from the ancient Mystical Order of The Sages better known as the Enlightened Sages. She was known as the child of the ancient Sage Farux and for some reason, they thought that they were inviting the male son of Farux. Upon her arrival, the base and tradition of this exclusive male-only society received a devastating shock to its foundation that changed it forever. Come and join the conversation now in progress...

- ***The Woman Sage who was supposed to be a man***

Sage Farinah stated to Chief Zazambu who refused to allow her entrance to their temple:

"I cannot understand your objection to a woman being a member of your circle even for a few hours or days. This is totally against reality and nature.

Since you claim that my invitation was a mistake and I must return to my place of origin, I would like you to know that if I stated that each one of you males here on earth is a mistake, and request your return to your place of origin, it would be back to the womb of a woman.

Your attitude and behavior is disrespectful to the source that housed you while you were a fetus and nourished you until you were in a position to be pushed out into this world where you are able to breathe on your own."

"How dare you reject me because I am a woman while ignoring that it was a woman's umbilical cord that gave you oxygen and fed you while in the womb!

Upon your independence from our umbilical cords, we fed you the necessary nutrients you needed from our breasts and gave you the comfort you needed to grow and today, you are saying that a woman is not worthy of sitting among you men?

My invitation was not a mistake. It is your lack of understanding of the vital role a woman plays in the universal laws of human creation that is the reason why we are at this impasse.

Your manmade reasoning to reject women from your circle of influence is the reason why energy and vibration conspired against this group and secretly concealed my gender during your invitation process, in order for me to be here to help you all remove the veil of ignorance from your bylaws so it can be in harmony with the laws of the Creator."

A woman from the village by the name of Shebba said; "You should have seen the faces of each of those so called learned men. You could not hear a whisper from any of them during Farinah's challenge of their status quo!" The ears of the women in the village were glued to every word that came from the woman Sage.

Shebba stated that one woman turned to another and said; "She must be directly connected to God," while another asked, "Is God a woman?"

8

Sage Farinah turned once more to the all-male group of elders of the Mystical Order of The Sages and said "Mother nature should send a bolt of lightning to destroy this anti-woman institution." Seconds later, the sky turned dark and nature gave the village elders the most beautiful dance of lightning and thunder.

The conversation was called to an immediate end by Chief Zazambu who rejected every word of Sage Farinah. He called an emergency gathering of all elders. That night, they all went to the top of the mountain for a special meeting. No such meeting had taken place in almost fifty years. The villagers were very concerned about the topic and the reason for such an emergency gathering of the wise men, because they understood and feared the vindictive Chief Zazambu.

The wise men got their invitation from the drumming that came from the top of the mountain. The special drumming sound informed the wise men and their understudies to immediately drop what they were doing and to come to the top of the holy mountain.

It was three days of intense philosophical debates and challenges to tradition. Only those in attendance were privileged to the process and results.

On the fourth day, the villagers saw a white smoke coming from the Holy Mountain indicating that the meeting ended. All the wise men from the various villages came down from the mountain and called for an extraordinary meeting that all villages must attend. Chief Sage Zazambu objected to the voting results and refused to attend. The following Sunday, all the sages from the villages took their seats in the temple except for Chief Zazambu whose chair remained empty. Chief Zazambu did not allow even one person from his village to attend the special, extraordinary event.

The villagers' curiosity was so strong that words were not necessary to feel the vibration that was being transmitted among each of them.

The Ceremony began with Senior Elder Sage Wantunak lighting the various candles and asking for the pure oil that was specially prepared by one of the initiated. No women were allowed to participate.

Upon reading of the bylaws and calling upon the bygone Sages and inviting the spiritual world to enter the temple of the Mystical Order of The Sages, an unexpected turn of events took place.

Chief Wantunak opened the ceremony with the following words that echoed for miles.

"We gather here today to announce a decision made by the Enlightened Sages of our villages that is going to have an everlasting effect on our tradition.

- We acknowledge and have respected for centuries Mother Earth (Gaia).

- We acknowledge the power and the presence of the sun from which our plants convert light energy into chemical energy to process their activities.

- We understand the importance of pure unpolluted water, in our search for the fountain of youth.

- We respect the energy beneath our rivers and those above and we bow to the hands that wrote the codes that set those energies in motion."

- We are aware for centuries of the role that the moon plays in creating the waves of the ocean and its effect on many phases of our lives.

- However, in our search for knowledge, wisdom and understanding, we have failed to acknowledge and respect the incubator that is responsible for maintaining the proper energy and vibration necessary for the development and delivery of each living human soul on planet earth; *woman.*

- We have listened to the prophetic words of Sage Farinah and have concluded among ourselves that the wisest Sage known to us today, including all of our bygone elders, is Sage Farinah.

After those words were spoken, the entire village could feel the negative energy and vibration coming hundreds of miles from the Village of Chief Zazambu.

Six men walked through the crowd and lifted Sage Farinah unto a Chariot and with three on either side, lifted the Chariot on their shoulders and walked towards Chief Wantunak. Upon her arrival at the center of the temple, these words were spoken:

- Today, we are going to add one more positive acknowledgement to our list, and that is, the divinity within each woman on planet earth by appointing Sage Farinah the Grand Master of the Mystical Order of The Sages better known as the *Enlightened Sages*.

She was escorted to the empty seat of the Grand Master and the proper regalia were placed on her.

The specially prepared oil was placed on her third eye and sprinkled on her feet and hands. She was now being addressed as the Anointed One or Goddess Farinah.

Women present from the various villages hugged and kissed each other with a passion never seen before. The differences among villagers disappeared instantly and a woman's rightful place among spiritual and religious groups was sealed.

The Anointed One accepted her status as Grand Master by saying, "Many Sages have argued that women had never been and could never be ordained since they were physically, mentally and spiritually inferior to men. Today, I call for the awakening of the Sage that is sleeping inside every woman to rise up and claim her rightful position as equal to any males on planet earth."

Goddess Farinah continued by saying; "The worst curse any person can commit, is to abuse and destroy mentally, physically and spiritually a women." To support her point, she stated that, "the Creator (God) trusted and anointed a woman with the task to protect the approximately nine month developmental process of a fetus until it is ready to be severed from its umbilical cord and breathe on its own."

From that day forward, every year there was a three-day celebration where the spirits of the ancestors were remembered, as well as the first woman Grand Master of the *Enlightened Sages*.

Sage Zazambu continued to refuse to participate in any such celebrations, and did not allow members of his village to attend.

In fact, he terminated all relationships with all villages who acknowledged the Sagehood of Goddess Farinah.

Chapter 3

During Goddess Farinah's reign as The Grand Master of the Mystical Order of The Sages, she conducted classes on nature and the universe. At one such class she was asked if there was other life in the Universe. She answered by saying that our ability to see each other coupled with our rational minds are perhaps the greatest obstacles man faces in understanding what life is...

• *Life from a Cosmic Perspective*

Goddess Farinah traveled the spiritual dimensions, sharing in the physical world her understanding of the spiritual and universal laws. She maintained the purity of her intellect and relationship with nature by eliminating, as much as possible, all things to do with human laws and ways of life.

She adopted her living and behavioral principles from the animal kingdom. She studied the Bonobo Apes and concluded that Apes are proven to be man's closest relative. She even discovered that young bonobos and children manage emotions in a similar fashion.

She was very much in love with the way ants build colonies and how they shared their workload without conflict or competition, which is one of man's primary downfalls.

One day Goddess Farinah brought together a group of young villagers who demonstrated a high level of intelligence and were ready to be groomed for Sagehood.

She started her communication with the group by saying; "Do not allow the limitation of your vision to conclude that if something or someone does not look like you, walks on two feet and has the ability to reason like you, that life does not exist within that which you are seeing or cannot see with your naked eyes.

When you look at each other, allow your knowledge of the Universal Laws to teach you that the physical body is nothing but a vessel for Energy and Vibration."

The Anointed One further stated "Within the frame of a human body, are trillions of cells working effortlessly to keep us in tune with the Creator's code, also referred to as, the Laws of Nature."

She asked the group to: "Always acknowledge that the energy and vibration within humans are the same energy and vibration within plants, fire, air and all other things that is visible and invisible to the human naked eyes."

Everyone understood better when she said "The shape of a tree, a bird or the various colors of crystal water around the world, are the manifestation of energy and vibration…everything is energy and vibration!"

The Anointed One told the young future leaders that; "When you remove a green fruit from a tree and leave it on your table for a few days and it starts to ripen, if it was dead or lifeless, it would stay green, therefore, life is everywhere." "Life force does not have any shape or form; it fits into everything and anything."

"I acknowledge the presence of life that exists within hurricanes, earthquake and rainbows. I also recognize the life force that keeps our planet earth and other cosmic planets from crashing into each other." Sage Farinah told the group never to forget that: "The Atoms, Nitrogen, Carbon and Oxygen within human beings came from the bowel of those stars that collapsed and spread their Atoms, Nitrogen, Carbon and Oxygen throughout the galaxy."

"Since the Atoms, Nitrogen, Carbon and Oxygen within man are the same that exist in the galaxy, we should be able to communicate effortlessly with the outer world by understanding how our entire body is intertwined with the life force elements on earth and in the galaxy."

Sage Farinah turned to a few of the women present and stated "There is no evidence that when the Creator wrote the code for the creation of life, that he favored the male over the female. On the contrary, the creation of a child takes 50% code from the male (sperm) and 50% from a female (egg) to create either a male or female child."

One of the seekers of knowledge asked the Anointed One what was her main passion and she said, *"To abolish or open to women, all Male organizations and institution, especially religious and political ones.*

My reason for that statement is: I believe that it is those All-Male groups and religious institutions that are the foundation for the negative treatment of women.

I noticed that wherever women hold decision-making positions in local organizations and religious institutions, they are also respected in the home and communities. Some are worshipped both by males and females alike."

The Anointed One looked sad when she shared her recollection of a trip where she noticed, young girls being forced into marriage at an early age. She said, "Those little girls were being sold by their parents and if they disobeyed, death by the hands of their families could be the punishment inflicted in order to keep face."

"I could not understand why the Creator's Universal Code for existence is so balanced and equal, while man-made code for coexistence is so unequal.

Women must realize that the reason they are in such a terrible position is because of the fact that men feel that if it is okay for religious institutions to exclude women from leadership, it's then okay for them to have all male leadership in their villages and in key decision- making positions, including being the masters of their homes.

Let us unite and change this misconception about women, but while we are doing so, we should not create exclusive women groups where men are excluded while women are trying to integrate all men's groups. There is a great need for the genders to heal and unite in love, forgiveness and respect."

Chapter 4

Farinah was almost one hundred and twenty five (125) years old with the body and mental alertness of a twenty five (25) year old person, and all those who were in her presence asked her to share with them the secret to the fountain of youth.

• *The Fountain of Youth*

"My understanding of nature as the force behind my ability to control the aging process has eluded many of you.+ Also, watching and documenting the various eating habits of the world's strongest and oldest animals, was fundamental in helping me create a diet that revealed to me the secret code behind a youthful look at any age."

Farinah's teaching was in the form of questions and answers (Q&A) which helps each person to learn at their own pace. Once learned, it becomes internalized forever. Each student became The Master of The Sage Within.

Goddess Farinah stated: "Another secret to my longevity and youthful looks is my understanding that carnivorous animals do not eat dead flesh. They capture their prey live and only eat when they were hungry. Man on the other hand, eats at every opportunity he gets.

Therefore, I refuse to eat dead animals… My vegetarian diet is fresh and alive!

I gained all my dietary knowledge from my three months stay in the jungle with a team of wise men from my surrounding villages."

17

"We observed and documented the various plants each animal ate. We even noticed the specific plants animal eat if they are not feeling well and the fast recovery they go through.

Armed with such knowledge, the entire team was able to go back to their domain and share their experiences which encouraged the decision by all villages to become vegetarians."

The three-month experience in the jungle with Goddess Farinah observing animal behaviors and documenting the various medicinal plants led the Sages from the various villages to becoming medicinal Doctors, sometimes referred to as Voodoo or Obeah man.

"Many of those great Sages who went with me into the jungle for three months abused the true teaching and created medicinal remedies for every conceivable disease.

They created special baths for the conception of a child.

They had medicinal solution for relationships and they even had solutions for good crop season."

Goddess Farinah's philosophy for longevity spread throughout India, China and Far Eastern villages who mastered her teachings.

Villages who abandoned the ancient teaching of Sage Farinah are witnessing the acceleration of the aging process.

Let us continue to listen to The Anointed One sharing her wisdom. "There is no doubt that man as a whole, cannot be trusted with making the right decisions to implement that which is good for mankind on a long term sustainable basis."

"Women, who the Creator entrusted and ordained to be the only bearer of human life, are the ones whose internal motherly instinct brought an aura of peace and tranquility among the various villages.

When the male species on planet earth are educated from an early age about the divinity of women and the important role we play in influencing the fetus inside of the womb, then, and only then, will men make sure that pregnant women are kept in a positive and peaceful state of mind?

Women, on the other hand, must learn from an early age that we all live 24/7 within our bodies and everything we put inside of it during pregnancy will be shared with the child within. The music we listen to and our state of mind has a direct effect on the child within."

The Anointed One concluded this gathering by saying. "In our search for the Fountain of Youth, we all should follow the eating habits of some of the strongest and most powerful animals on planet earth, the majority of who are vegetarians.

The majority of carnivorous animals do not eat dead meat. They hunt and eat their prey fresh and alive. Man is one of the few mammals that eat dead flesh! "If you want to die young at an old age, do not eat that which will eat you!"

Chapter 5

Sage Farinah's popularity spread to the four corners of the earth. Spiritual leaders from all walks of life journeyed for weeks and months to be at the feet of Sage Farinah. She is referred to more often as Goddess Farinah by those who adored her wisdom, knowledge and understanding of planet earth and the cosmos. Twelve wise men travelled from all parts of the world in search of answers to which they feel that only Goddess Farinah holds the answer. The first question asked of The Anointed One by an Indian yogi was, "is there a God?"

- ### *Is There A God?*

A silence instantly fell over the entire temple. Goddess Farinah closed her eyes and for a few minutes, it seems like her body was there, but her soul was traveling.

Her immediate answer was, "Your question is obvious. You have lost your birth innocence that gave you unobstructed direct communication with the Creator's Universal Laws.

Your question is also based on a traditional religious concept of a creator who looks like man.

To find and understand God, you must come to the conclusion that the Creator only speaks one language and not thousands of languages and dialects that are only understood by the users of that particular language or dialect.

The Galaxy or cosmic world does not use languages or dialects; it uses mathematical formulas that are useable and interchangeable among all planets and stars."

"Once you understand the Universal Laws of Nature, you will immediately eliminate the existence of a God that helps us out based on prayers or generosity at any given moment.

During my 125 years on planet earth, and during my short experience of the creation process when a sperm and an egg came together that led to that great internal explosion that is responsible for my being here today, I cannot recall the interference of a God in that process.

The code for the creation of a human being is written and all it needs to be activated is the presence of thousands of sperms in pursuit of a fertile egg that is ready to open its door to one of those challengers.

If you think that man is intelligent and smart, then, what would you call those cells within a woman's egg that knows how to put together all the necessary parts that will grow into fingers, toes, legs, arms, eyes, brain, taste, smell, touch? I call them the living Intelligent (God) in action."

Goddess Farinah posed the question to a group of wise men with whom she was reasoning: "How can you be more intelligent than the process that created you?"

She made it clear that: "If the creative process of nature's Universal Laws is referred to as God, then, yes, there is a God."

She made a very important point by saying, "If God is meant to be a physical person who is responsible for granting favors and support, we would be unable to predict anything because that God could change it at will. There is no evidence that such interference is happening."

21

"The Cosmic mathematical process will give the same results every time it is applied without any Godly intervention."

Sage Farinah explained that; "There is a God or Gods who wrote the codes of the Universe and that God or Gods are totally involved in the continuous expansion of the Galaxy. Once those codes are activated, it just works. Nothing is unconnected in the Universe" she said.

Everything is connected, from the constant breathing of oxygen to the exhaling of carbon dioxide. The cause and effect theory is constantly in motion even if we are not aware of it.

Another powerful code that exists in the universe is our ability to mix different elements together and create a third element that never existed in such a form.

Man further has the ability to reshape and change earth as much as he wants, with one crucial understanding, that is, if in the process man violates crucial mathematical formulas of the laws of nature, then, nature will turn around and eliminate man from the face of the earth by introducing diseases or an environment that is not sustainable for human existence.

Then, planet earth will begin to repair the ills created by man and start the process all over again, but this time, without the presence of the most destructive creature on planet earth, man!"

When Chief Zazambu heard of Goddess Farinah's philosophy of God, he was furious because he uses religion as his foundation to control his entire village.

He explained to his villagers that he has direct connection with God and for the Anointed One to cast doubts on such ideology, was not welcoming.

Many months later, while meditating in her temple, The Anointed One received a surprising visit from one of the ladies of Chief Zazambu's village whom she had not seen in years.

She welcomed her and they both sat down. The Anointed One then asked her; "What urgency brought you here to this village in total violation of Chief Zazambu orders?"

She replied, "Chief Zazambu is dying from a rare disease that none of the wise men of the village can cure. They have heard of the great healing work you have been doing, so they secretly sent me for advice as to what we can do to save Chief Zazambu's life."

After a long discussion about the symptoms of Chief Zazambu's illness, Goddess Farinah recalled a special herb she learned about during her three months expedition into the deep jungle studying the various animals' behaviors and eating habits.

She summoned two of her leading herbalists and jungle experts to go in search of a particular medicinal plant she named The 'Invisible Healer'.

Upon their successful return, she extracted the oil from the plant and gave it to the visitor with one stipulation; "Do not tell Chief Zazambu who gave you this remedy."

The visitor returned to her village and gathered the elders who asked her to take the trip, and gave them the medicine.

For seven days the Chief was fed the oil and each day the villagers were able to see a drastic improvement of his health.

Within nine days, Chief Zazambu came from the bowel of death back to a healthy earthly being.

Approximately six months later, The Anointed One, Goddess Farinah, announced the date for their fourth annual celebration and Chief Zazambu made it clear to his entire village that they should not even think of asking for his permission to attend.

The day of the event, Chief Zazambu noticed that his entire village gathered in preparation of a long journey which no one informed him about. He called an emergency meeting of the elders and asked the question, "Where are the villagers going and how come I was excluded from such decision?"

Chief Elder Makubu stated; "We are going to visit The Anointed One, Goddess Farinah." Chief Zazambu shouted, "Didn't I forbid each one of you from attending her annual event?"

Elder Makubu answered, "We are not going to participate in the event" and he purposely paused, knowing well what the next question was going to be.

Then, the question was asked as predicted. "Why is the entire village going there?"

Makubu delivered the devastating answer, "To give thanks to The Anointed One, Goddess Farinah, for preparing the medicine that saved your life!" Chief Zazambu fell into his chair and looked into the sky like he was in a different world. He did not answer or repeated another word.

The elders quietly walked out one by one. They gathered the villagers and went their merry way. The new arrivals were welcomed for the first time, but all were disappointed about the empty chair of Chief Zazambu over the years.

In the middle of the celebration, silence came over the entire event. It was so quiet; you could hear the sound of a grasshopper. It was the arrival of Chief Zazambu who came to occupy his empty seat.

Chief Zazambu during an intermission asked The Anointed One, what was the name of the herb she gave and she answered," In our village it is called Ganja and in your village, you call it Marijuana." He was shocked because he heard so much of the healing properties of the Ganja plant, but never gave it any serious attention.

The Anointed One further stated, "It is the oil from the plant that is more powerful than smoking it. Ganja, Moringa and Aloe plants are three of nature's wonder medicines."

Chief Zazambu was asked to close the ceremony. He delivered a powerful statesman-like presentation. Zazambu will go down in history for a statement he made that night that is quoted all over the world; *"A Person Should Never Be Judged Based on Their Gender, but on Their Ability to Deliver That Which Is Promised."*

He closed his presentation by saying, "Yes, there is a God that is full of energy and vibration and God is mathematically precise in his outcome!"

Chapter 6

The Anointed One, Goddess Farinah, journeyed to all four corners of the earth. Her gatherings drew the initiated and neophytes alike. She recalled the gathering of women from around the world, who visited her in search of her interpretation of what is love and why she was not married! She asked the audience what does love have to do with marriage?

What Love Has To Do With Marriage?

The Anointed One explained to the group of women that there are two types of love. There is "unconditional love" and there is "let's make a deal love" and she proceeded to explain the difference between both.

"You usually find unconditional love between parents and children. This type of love usually is not broken regardless of how loving or unloving that child is.

A child could be the most vicious criminal and for some reason, the bond especially between the child and mother, is still there.

Unconditional love sometimes is a one way relationship, where one person will continue to have and show love and affection towards another, even though the other person has ceased to show any such love or affection."

The Anointed One stated: "During many of my discussions with individuals who have shown unconditional love, it is usually in an abusive relationship where the male is domineering, possessive and physically abusive.

In those cases, the male shows no sign of affection, even though the female genuinely shows love and affection towards her mate."

Goddess Farinah told the congregation of women that; "The refusal to acknowledge women as equal by major religious and social institutions has had a direct effect on how women are treated at home and in their communities."

"My meeting with abusive males from around the world told me basically the same thing. If a man is the head of powerful decision making groups and religious organizations, then, he must and should be the decision maker of his home.

Based on the above statement, I believe that secret societies, village chiefs, religious institutions and other male-only groups, who refuse to acknowledge the divinity and equality of a woman, are directly or indirectly responsible for the unwelcome image women are experiencing around the world."

She got the attention of every woman present when she said : "Let's make a deal love is where two people say to each other *I love you* but what they really mean is this, *I will love you, if you love me. The day you stop loving me, I too will stop loving you.*

Let's make a deal love is the foundation on which many marriages and relationships are based.

It's an emotional love that is not anchored on anything besides emotions. That is why I asked, What does love have to do with marriage?

Baaku was the youngest female in the audience and her question was, "Why are men allowed to have so many wives?"

Goddess Farinah meditated on this one and then replied. "The low birth rate of males and the high survival rate of females, created an imbalance among male and female in the villages. In order to allow other women to experience marriage and child bearing, polygamy was created and practiced legally."

The Anointed One shared her discovery of other types of marriages. She stated: "I discovered the existence of Polyandry, whereby a woman takes two or more husbands at the same time. I noted that the Himalayans had about 53 societies that practiced polyandry."

Fraternal polyandry was traditionally practiced among *Tibetans* in *Nepal*, parts of *China* and part of northern India, in which two or more brothers are married to the same wife, with the wife having equal sexual access to them. Baaku understood the rationalization behind polygamy, but wanted to find out the reason for polyandry.

The Anointed One stated: "It was explained to me that in the Himalayan Mountains polyandry is related to the scarcity of land; the marriage of all brothers in a family to the same wife, allows family land to remain intact and undivided."

The Anointed One seems to have tears in her eyes when she speaks about her experience in India. "I cannot understand the marriage of young girls under the age of 13, and the physical abuse many of them experience, especially the wanton abandonment of girl children at birth." In a broken and tearful voice she asked, "What can a 13 year old know about love?"

The entire gathering of women seemed like they were on a journey with The Anointed One while she was regurgitating her experience, because there was not 'one dry eye' in the audience.

Baaku seemed to be on a quest for information that is why she asked The Anointed One why she never got married. Goddess Farinah after hearing the question, brought a smile of liberation on her face that said, I have being waiting for that question.

"The truth is, from my conception until today, I have been occupied in keeping active the channel of communication between myself and the universal laws. If I start to occupy myself with family daily activities, my focus would have changed and my ability to stay in tune with my universal spirituality would have been lost over time.

I do believe that each one of us has a role to play and my role is not to have a husband or a few children, but to adopt as many souls as my own and share with them the importance of a balanced life.

Over the last 125 years, I have saved thousands of lives. I have given birth to internal peace and happiness to both males and females from all walks of life and I have elevated the status of women around the world.

I taught millions of individuals how to find the fountain of youth by adopting a healthy lifestyle diet and I have helped thousands to be good stewards of mother earth.

Marriage and childbearing would have robbed all those thousands of people of my time and spirituality. I know I am fulfilling my destiny by accepting the role that was handed to me by The Universal Laws of Life."

Baaku walked towards The Anointed One, hugged her and whispered in her ears, *"thank you mother Farinah!"*

Chapter 7

*The Anointed One was on an expedition to Egypt where she was
supposed to meet indigenous healers. Their reputations were
mixed. Many feared them and others were amazed by their
magical powers. She was more fascinated about their strong love
for nature and vegetarian diet. The Chief Sage of the Village was
a woman by the name of Chioma. Upon the arrival of The
Anointed One to Egypt, she was being greeted as Sage Chioma by
many of the Chief Sages of the various villages.*

• *Who Is Sage Chioma?*

The Anointed one was very mystified for the first time in her life.
"How can anyone confuse me with someone else?" She was more
desirous in getting to Sage Chioma's village/temple with the least
amount of delay.

Goddess Farinah recalled the five-day journey it took to reach Sage
Chioma's Village.

Upon her arrival, the entire village looked at her in awe. Some put
their hands on their mouths so as to prevent themselves from
screaming. Others put their hands on their heads like they just
witnessed something amazing or inexplicable. While some opened
their eyes so wide, it seemed like they were about to come out of
the sockets.

When The Anointed One saw Sage Chioma for the first time, she
stopped in her tracks. Sage Chioma seemed to be a carbon copy of
her. One could easily say that they are identical twins.

They both walked towards each other and attempted to hug but the energy and electric shock between them was too strong. It was an experience never seen before between two human beings.

The two Sages looked at each other in amazement. "You are me and I am you. We are one person in two bodies, how could that be?" Said Sage Chioma.

After hours of amazement, confusion and questions, the two Sages sat down for a meeting of the minds in search of the question at hand and that is, "where did they both come from?"

After hours of sharing background information, a light went on for the Anointed One.

She told Sage Chioma, "I recall stories in the village about my mother having twins and my father, Sage Farux, gave my twin sister to a Sage by the name of Damba in return for precious stones.

It was told that Sage Damba could not have any children and my father, Sage Farux, made a promise that if the heavens blessed him with twins, he would share the blessing with him, Sage Damba.

Sage Chioma whispered in the ears of The Anointed One and said, "We are sisters, Sage Damba is my father. Now I know that he is not my biological father. He told me that my mother was from another village, and she died right after my delivery."

The Anointed one responded by saying, "I have travelled the world and listen to so many children stolen, sold or given away, who never had the chance to meet their biological parents. Many never learned that their parents are really not their biological parents.

We are blessed to have found each other and now able to unite with our parents as one family."

Sage Damba was on an expedition and upon his return he got the greatest shock of his life. He was unable to differentiate between the twins. He was so amazed and shocked, he blacked out and fainted.

After his recovery, he gathered the elders and had a meeting and the result of that meeting was the following:

Sage Damba admitted to the elders; "Sage Chioma was actually adopted and Sage Farinah is her biological twin sister."

Sage Damba decided to step down as the Chief Elder and turned over all authority to Sage Chioma.

They celebrated the reunion of the two sisters and they ate and dined all night.

Everyone then went to bed to prepare for the next day's spiritual journey that The Anointed One had prepared.

About 4:00 am that morning, they heard the most beautiful songs coming from a group of birds who never, ever, are awake that time of the morning.

Out of curiosity, the villagers came out and they noticed that the moon was full and shinning on Sage Damba's tent.

Sage Chioma decided to enter her father's tent to share the wonderful blessing they were experiencing, only to realize that he had passed away and the birds and the moon were welcoming him into the spiritual world.

Sage Chioma came out and hugged her sister and refused to let her go. What was most amazing, they both noticed that the electrical shock that kept them apart was gone; they were able to bond physically.

After the cremation of Sage Damba the following day, Sage Chioma was going through her father's files. She came across an envelope with her name on it with the official wax seal of the village. She proceeded to open it and the following were the contents of the letter:

"My darling daughter, you are reading this letter because I am no longer here on earth with you. Having you in my life was the most precious thing I have had and it is time for you to know certain truths.

I am not your biological father. The great Sage Farux, the father of The Anointed One, Sage Farinah, is your father and Sage Farinah is your twin sister. Your father will explain to you in details how you came to be with me.

My daughter Chioma, the helper Kibibi who visited us once or twice per year that you loved so much, is actually your biological mother and she is my sister.

I am actually your uncle and the uncle of Sage Farinah.

Please continue to love your mother. She did not give you up for adoption. Such decisions are only made by the Chief Sage of the village.

I have never seen The Anointed One, but I was told that she is your identical twin, and I am looking forward to you both bonding.

33

I am over 175 years old and I really enjoyed my physical presence on earth. I am looking forward to my transition wherever it takes me.

Your youthful look at 125 years is due to the medicinal herbs your mother brought for you that were discovered by your sister Sage Farinah.

Farewell, may the blessings of the Gods be with you and everyone else until we meet again, in the spiritual world from whence we all came."

Chapter 8

Sage Chioma shared the content of the letter with her sister Farinah and they both learned some truth that was hidden from them all their lives. Sage Chioma turned to her sister and asked, "Can you explain to me your understanding of death and the afterlife?"

- ## *What Is Death and After Life?*

The Anointed One said, "Is there really such a thing as death? Or is it our lack of understanding the transition of things, from one state to another?"

If we can find the answer to a Caterpillar's metamorphosis where a worm sheds its skin and becomes a butterfly, then, we could better understand what death is.

"What is not human like with butterflies is that, butterflies do not provide parental care for their offspring, and in most cases, by the time the caterpillars hatch from the eggs, the adult butterfly that laid the eggs is either dead or has moved on."

Goddess Farinah told her sister; "I had the privilege to share precious moments with Zoroaster, the founder of the ancient religious order called Zoroastrianism. One of his deepest beliefs is expressed in this quote, *"If there were no death, there will be no religion."*

"According to him and many others, religious and spiritual institutions evolved in their search of the answer to one question, what happens to humans after death?"

35

"The day we find what exists after the spirit leaves the body, my sister Chioma, everyone's religion, medicine man, fortune teller and Obeah man, will no longer exist.

We must be grateful to be here, thanks to death. If it was not for the passing of those who have gone before us, there would not be room on earth to accommodate us all.

Chioma interjected by saying. "It is so challenging after spending so many beautiful years with family and friends and developing a dependency on each other, just to be left with memories, this is one of nature's secrets we must master."

Sage Chioma said: "We noticed that when certain birds die, the others fly around that bird wishing it goodbye."

"We witness Gorillas and other animals who get depressed after the death of their mother with whom they have developed a strong bond."

Chioma said to her sister, "I recalled while in mother's womb, how I was able to travel spiritually and was surprised when I left that environment and was now on my own. What was more amazing, I never recalled interacting with you in mother's womb."

Chioma asked Farinah, "Can we say that the transition from mother's womb to our present physical state is a form of death?"

The Anointed One smiled and said, "Can we also say that the plant we eat, which is now being transformed from one state into another, is dying when we remove it from the tree or earth? It is no longer attached to the roots of that tree or the soil of life."

"Does a fruit or medicinal plant go through a dying process while we are masticating it in our mouth, or can we say that it actually dies when we digest it?

Since we have no knowledge of what happens beyond death, but based on solid earthly metamorphosis like that of the *Caterpillar to a Butterfly*, we can say that death is an ongoing transformational process which has no finality. Its purpose is to take us to the next level of existence, to live, learn and transform into a being of elevated intellect and spirituality."

Chioma answered her sister's eloquent explanation of what death could mean by saying that, "Our lack of understanding the fundamental process of nature, creates so many speculations in search of answers, that it's probably complicating a simple answer that is eluding us all."

Chioma further stated: "Since no one has ever returned from the dead to explain what is beyond death, speculations will continue to be part of our daily conversation."

The Anointed One interjected: "I have met many a person who can accurately speak about things that happened hundreds of years before their birth, which proved that they were here before, but no one can tell us what death is about and what exists on the other side of life."

"Sister Chioma, do you know that there are cultures, where when the King dies, that many of his slaves and servants are buried alive with him?"

Chioma said yes and further expanded by saying; "I have witnessed during the prediction of bad weather or harvest season, where children were sacrificed to please the Gods in order to prevent the bad prediction from coming true."

The Anointed One shared with her sister about the three months she spent in the deep jungle studying animals and the bonds developed among them, which are similar to human bonds.

We humans have developed strong family bonds with our horses, dogs and other animals, especially when we became strict vegetarians. Upon their passing, we feel the same loss similar to when one of our loved ones pass away.

Chioma's eyes became tearful, recalling the relationship she had with her white stallion horse by the name of Whitey. Chioma spoke passionately about the great friendship that existed between the both of them. They were able to communicate with each other and predict what the other was experiencing or needed.

Chioma told her sister, "Even though his passing was almost 10 years ago, I can still remember our daily ride to nowhere. Our playful moments and the time I got hurt and Whitey rode back to the Village and galloped like a wild horse until he got my father's attention.

My father followed him to the place where I was located, he saved my life.

Death leaves only memories to hold on to and if one is not strong, it can take away your will to live."

The Anointed One feels that our state of mind is a contributing factor to one's good or bad health. She acknowledges the brain as the master of our life.

Sage Chioma added to the conversation by saying, "You are what you think. If you think that you are great, nothing anyone else says will affect you. If you believe that you do not deserve better, then, you will accept any status into which you are placed."

Sister Farinah, "We are living proof that women can be leaders and execute those leadership positions with dignity and respect."

"Let us remember fondly all those who came before us, both humans and animals that played a positive and loving role in our lives. Farewell until we meet in that place from whence we came."

Chapter 9

The word spread about the twins and their mystical powers. Their daily activity was to serve the long line of families who brought their sick loved ones for blessing and healing. The lines were so long, that many of them had to be in the sun for hours. The sisters were asked on many occasions, what was the secret to their high rate of success with some of the most incurable diseases.

- ## *What Are Our Curable Secrets?*

The Anointed One and her sister Sage Chioma became an inseparable duo who worked together since their reunion.

Chioma laughed with her sister Farinah and said, "If they only knew the simple secrets to good health." Sage Farinah answered by saying: "We should no longer keep those secrets to ourselves; let us share them with the masses so they can share it with others." "This will lead to healthy societies, and many of them can experience our goal for everyone and that is, to die young at a very old age!"

During that afternoon, The Anointed One asked the visitors the following questions: "Why do you think we start our healing process at 10:00 a.m.? Why do we refuse to have our sessions in a more covered area?"

Chioma answered her sister's question by saying to the visitors, "We do so because we have discovered that the majority of your sicknesses and diseases are due to the lack of Vitamin D and the Sun is the main source for vitamin D."

"Instead of going back to your villages and hide from the Sun, every morning you should put on the least amount of clothing and sit in the Sun for at least 30 to 45 minutes.

We call this, our daily morning Sun bath. We also discovered that the darker your skin is, the more sunlight you need to create the proper amount of Vitamin D.

The second most powerful cure is the pureness of the quality of the water you drink. Make sure that you get your water directly from the mountains. Try not to leave your drinking water open because flying insects can leave their eggs in that water and when you drink it, you are infected with diseases."

There was an elder among the crowd by the name of Chief Aris, who was absorbing every word coming from the lips of the two Sage sisters, he then stood up and with a voice that could be heard for miles, he said, "Your knowledge of the human body and the various medicinal cures is impressive.

I am166 years old and I have been studying herbs and their medicinal properties for over 145 years, and one thing I observed, animals usually have a bowel movement shortly after they eat.

We human sometimes do not have a bowel movement for days after eating a big feast day after day. I have discovered a few herbs if you drink them as tea, they will give you an immediate bowel movement. Also, if you put those teas in water and leave them in the Sun, Mother Nature will extract their medicinal qualities for you."

I come from a village called Sunfired because we only eat food that is cooked by the sun."

"No one in our village has ever eaten any food that is cooked by fire, and that is the secret for the disease- free lifestyle and longevity of our villagers living over 200 years."

Chief Aris went on to explain that "It is important to get rid of food before it starts to rot and decompose inside of our bodies, creating toxic waste and disease."

He said that: "Within a few hours of eating, the intelligence within our body extracts that which it needs and the rest is waste to be eliminated from our body. If we can remove those wastes as fast as possible, then, we can improve our health and longevity."

Chief Aris shared a fact that everyone was shocked about. He asked, "Are you aware of the fact that our small intestines, where the food processing takes place, is almost 2,700 square feet? Can you imagine the amount of food that can be stored in the human body? Can you imagine having 2,700 square feet of decomposed food in your system? Can you imagine the smell of decomposed liquid food? That smell is the reason for bad human breath and body odors!"

Chief Aris, the medicinal doctor closed by saying; "Each region and village has their own herbs that does the same thing.

Find out which medicinal herbs help you to speed up your bowel movement and take it at least once per month. It will help you *To Die Young at an Old Age.*"

Another mystic by the name of Ruach stood up and spoke about the medicinal properties of music.

Ruach said; "I have witnessed people from all walks of life that lost their memories, their ability to walk or talk, regain those functions through the various types of music played for them.

I have met wise men in villages who have become Masters at using music to heal the sick. They know the exact type of drum or musical instrument to play, in order to heal the various types of sicknesses.

They told me that they are able to awaken the Sage Within, also known as The Doctor Within.

These musical wise men are using certain musical notes that stimulate the energy and vibration within. It allows our internal intelligence to function at their maximum capacity."

Mystic Ruach said; "Certain music can put the most awakened person to sleep due to its relaxation qualities.

Other types of music can put you in a trance to the point that you start to speak in other languages of which you have no knowledge.

Based on the beat of music, it can put you in a state of joy and happiness or, it can stimulate action and violence from within. Music is a stimulus that must be delivered carefully" said Mystic Ruach.

Sage Chioma recalled visiting, many years ago, the Laughing Sage whose discovery shows that laughter is the antidote for many of his villager's sadness, loneliness and sicknesses. Individuals were cured after they took a daily dose of laughter for a few days or weeks.

Chioma continued by saying; "Many adults who started to do childhood things like playing, sharing bygone memories with friends that bring on laughter, were able to experience great deal of happiness and joy that has eluded them for years.

It was amazing to see individuals with skin diseases and those suffering from sadness for many years, healed in a short period of time when they were placed in an environment that forced them to laugh and be cheerful."

The Anointed One added her comment by saying, "There is strong evidence that all adults should have daily childish moments in their life in order to have the good health and free spirit, like children.

It is when we assume family and social responsibilities that we stop doing the things that used to make us happy. We adopt a state of mind that reduces our daily happiness that contributes to our illnesses."

The Anointed One told the group, ***"You should never try to be an adult, remain a responsible child, regardless of your age!"***

Sage Chioma interjected by sharing with the group these facts; "I learned from an early age that I possess healing hands. When I lay my hands on someone, within minutes, that area becomes a burning inferno. I am able to cure many skin ailments and warts on people's bodies by penetrating those areas, by placing my heated hands on them.

I also noticed that I was able to help others who were suffering from body pains and inability to move their body parts by laying my hands on those areas until those persons could not bear the heat anymore."

"I repeated the process three to five times during each session. The success was amazing.

Based on those experiences, I decided to do an experiment many years ago on the power of hugging (touching) and came to the conclusion that from the moment of birth, until our last breath on earth, hugging conveys a feeling of love and security."

Chioma also discovered: "Hugging helps to stimulate pressure points on the body that trigger an internal energy and vibration process that fuels the entire body positively."

Chioma told her sister Farinah: "The most amazing thing about hugging is that it relaxes the muscles and stimulates circulation of the blood. Another benefit of hugging is that, those who hug each other a lot create trust among themselves."

The Anointed One thanked her sister for sharing such informative knowledge and told her that this interactive conversation triggered her memory about what she learned regarding sleep.

The Anointed One said; "Total darkness is the best environment for one to sleep. During a full moon, the animals that come out during full darkness, experience a behavior change.

Even though full moon is a beautiful scene, make sure your sleeping space is as dark as possible in order for your body to have the best sleep. Improper sleep patterns have a direct effect on aging. It is not the amount of sleep you get; it is the quality of sleep. I can get four hours sleep per day and feel rested and alert.

I take small quiet breaks during the day, which is great for the mind, body and soul."

Chapter 10

The Anointed One and her sister were entertaining three visiting guests who had made an appointment months before.

During their casual meeting and answering questions about their spirituality, their belief in the existence of God and their healing abilities, one of their loyal followers by the name of Sadiq, sent for The Anointed One. The messenger whispered in her ears that she must excuse herself urgently, and to tell the visitors that she will soon return.

She met Sadiq right outside the temple who informed her about his true identity and those of the three men she was meeting with.

- ## *Who Is Sadiq and The Three Visitors?*

It turned out that over the years, Chioma and Farinah's popularity spread so far and wide that it started to become a challenge to religious institutions around the world.

Unknown to them, they were being labeled Witches and Sorcerers. The various denominations came together to create a unified force to destroy once and for all, the evil force of The Anointed One and Sage Chioma.

Sadiq was one of 12 individuals who were sent to infiltrate their meetings and events, in order to gather evidence of their witchcraft activities and to identify all those who are trained to be Witches by the twin sisters.

After years of traveling with the group, Sadiq came to the conclusion that everything they teach and practice have been and can be duplicated by anyone, because it all has to do with the laws of nature.

Sadiq was now a true loyal follower who was informing The Anointed One that those three men were from three different religious institutions who were gathering evidence to have them prosecuted and burned as witches and sorcerers.

After meeting with Sadiq, Sage Farinah asked that the entire villagers gather around the bonfire like they did for their monthly village mastermind meetings.

The Anointed One returned to the temple with a smile on her face, and asked her sister and the three visitors to follow her since there was a short change of plan.

Just when they were about to start their ceremony, there was an unexpected visitor, Chief Zazambu.

Sage Chioma's curiosity was getting the better of her.

Her sister had been abruptly called away from their meeting and upon her return, she terminated the meeting and called a monthly meeting that was not scheduled for another seven days and, in the process, Chief Zazambu appeared unannounced.

The Anointed One opened the ceremony, spoke, then she opened it to the visitors to ask whatever questions they wanted and anyone was obliged to answer. Well, the first question asked by the visitors was, what is the religious belief of the two sisters?

47

Sage Chioma was about to shock the entire villagers and visitors with her answers.

She said; "I am the *living* manifestation of God."

"Religion does not speak about a living God. Religion speaks about things that happened in the past and share that information with its members and those who want to listen to historical data.

Not only that I worship a living God, every breath I take, every living plant I eat and the water I drink is the manifestation of God.

All religions are bound by written documentations. Religious followers must obey those bygone written documents word for word. It leaves no room for new discovery or growth.

When I wake up every day and look up to the universe, I know that the Godly hands that wrote the codes to everything I see and know about the galaxy, is the same God who resides inside of me as living and intelligent cells."

Sage Chioma was on a spiritual role when she pointed out that God is the energy and vibration within every plant, animal, stone, human, water, air, oxygen, carbon dioxide. God is everywhere and in everything.

Regardless if you are a member of a religious institution or not, you cannot exist on Planet Earth without The Creator's presence. The Creator is everything we see and feel."

Sage Chioma gained the respect of her sister The Anointed One as a spiritual channel when she said; "My ancestors have warned me about those who might think I am a witch or sorcerer."

I refute witchcraft and all types of organized religions, even though I respect and will support their freedom to be, and hope they respect my freedom to my belief."

No one could stop Chioma that night.

Chioma said: "When I witness the wanton killing of humans due to religious differences, and the calling upon the various Gods for protection in times of wars, I often ask, where is the love and respect for human life that is embedded within those organized religious groups?"

Our goal is very clear; we are here to help save lives. We never create an environment that will cause hurt or destruction of another human being.

We do not burn or kill people because we disagree with their teaching or ideology.

If there is anyone among us today who disagree with our beliefs, should we vote right now, find them guilty and have them thrown into our bonfire that is now burning?

We teach people how to be the Master of The Sage Within and How to be the Master of The God Within, not to be the judge, jury and executioner against those who do not adhere to our way of life."

The Anointed One was shocked with the answers from her sister Chioma because she did not inform her about the motive and objective of the three visitors.

Chief Zazambu stood up and started clapping, which was followed by everyone else and faintly by the three visitors.

Chief Zazambu said; "I left my village to be here with you both because, I heard a rumor that there is a conspiracy to label you as witches and sorcerers.

I was sick and dying and every church leader came and prayed for me and many were helping me to meet my maker, God. To my surprise, The Anointed One's knowledge of God's Universal Laws was able to identify the proper medicinal plant and extracted the oil, which I took that cure me. I am alive thanks to The Anointed One.

I have never seen an evil act, thought or action from either of the sister Sages and anyone who accuses you both of being witches should be hung until their neck is Broken."

You should have seen the uneasiness of the three visitors. They started sweating and two of them opened their shirt collar, as if it was getting too tight around their neck.

No one informed the visitors or the elders that they knew Sadiq was sent to infiltrate the village by them.

That evening, the visitors were invited to a special ceremony in the temple and to their surprise; it was the initiation of Sadiq to the status of a Chief.

The three visitors never gave anyone the indication that they knew Sadiq; they kept that secret to themselves.

The Anointed One and her sister Sage Chioma never heard anymore threats of witchcraft against them but they knew that religious institutions did not agree with their spiritual views or inexplicable healing powers.

Chapter 11

Over the years, The Anointed One and Sage Chioma had heard of Mystics who had become Master Mysticmorphosists™. Both sisters decided to pack their bags and attend the world conference of Mystics and Sages to be held in Ethiopia. [Ethopia is formerly known as Abyssinia, derived from Habesh or Habesha is the native name for the country's inhabitants (while the country has been called "Ityopp'ya".]

- ## *Who Is A Mysticmorphosist™*

During their five days travel to the conference, The Anointed One and Sage Chioma were able to share information about their knowledge of various spiritual and universal beliefs. Please join their conversation in progress:

The Anointed One said to Chioma, "since man is made of energy and vibration, do you think that one hundred or a few thousand years from now, man will find a way to tap into any mind and listen into each other's thoughts?"

Chioma answered by saying, "That is a very interesting question."

"I was told many years ago by a Sage who became the Master of the human body that no two individuals have the same fingerprint pattern.

Therefore, to tap into any mind and listen into each other's thoughts, we are assuming that each person will have a unique energy and vibration code that is similar to fingerprints."

"The reason why I will agree with you that such discovery could be possible in the future as man evolves, is because everything happens in the mind.

We are what we think. We create our own reality based on what we think is true or false.

If man is able to find a way to identify the vibration or energy code of a person, and man is able to duplicate such code, then, one will be able to tap into any person's mind by discovering their vibration and energy's unique code."

Sage Farinah shared with her sister Chioma what she learned by being in the company of some Ancient Mystics.

"They told me of their observation of how many animals, fish and birds have the ability to go through a process called Metamorphosis. A great example is how a caterpillar is able to transform into a butterfly from a chrysalis.

Mystics have the potential to activate the Metamorphosis property that is sleeping in each one of us.

Having the ability to change our look or color instantly, to blend into our environment in order to avoid detection, is a phenomenon that has evaded man. This survival ability is within our reach, when we begin to use our spiritual mind, instead of our physical mind.

Master Mysticmorphosists are those Mystics who have learned how to master their energy, vibration and the intelligence within that enable them to change their features instantly."

"Many of them are able to communicate directly with the cells of their bodies, sometimes called the Intelligence God Within.

In the same way we can tell our mind to move our feet or hands; Mysticmorphosists are able to tell their cells to repair any internal part of their body that is damaged. They are Masters of their Mind, Body and Soul."

Sage Chioma was fascinated by her sister's explanation of a Mysticmorphosist. She was so excited that not only did she want to meet and learn from those Ancient Mystics who were going to be at the conference; she hope that at least one Mysticmorphosist would also be there.

The conversation between the sisters was so interesting that they themselves did not realize that they had been traveling for almost five days. They were a few hours away from the Ethiopian mountain by the name "Freedom," where Ancient Mystics and Sages were gathering to share their knowledge with each other, to help improve the positive energy and vibration in every corner of the world.

Upon their arrival, they observed hundreds of Mystics from all walks of life. The welcome they both received reminded them of past rejections. They were the only women present, at this all male Mystic gathering. The men did not know how to deal with the two female Sages.

One of the leading known Mystic at the gathering by the name of Kerani, called a meeting of a few of the decision makers and told them that he had the privilege of being in the company of the two female Sages and that he vouched for their authenticity.

Asiza, another Mystic who is highly respected among Mystics shared with the group that he personally knew the work of The Anointed One and Sage Chioma, even though he had never had the privilege of meeting them.

They voted to allow the sisters to attend, with a few Mystics objecting to any women participating in their events.

The Mystical world was about to unveil secrets on living in harmony with The Sage Within and how to obey the Laws of Nature in order to have peace within and without.

The ceremony started that evening with the gathering of all Mystics sitting in a semi-circle. Mystic Parajan stood up and welcomed the group. He said; "Let us start the ceremony with a symbol of peace."

He took off his scarf from around his shoulder and folded it, opened it again and a white dove flew out. He was applauded and the ceremony began.

There was no agenda: therefore, it was open to anyone who wanted to do a presentation since they were all Mystic Masters in their own rights.

Mystic Desmond walked to the center of the group and the entire audience was silent. When he speaks, everyone listens.

Mystic Desmond opened his presentation by saying, "The first thing a new born baby does after leaving the womb, is to take his or her first breath and the last thing that child does before departing mother earth, is to exhale its last breath. Therefore, the only thing that exists between life and death is our breath."

"We take approximately 21 thousand breaths per day" said Mystic Desmond.

"Conscious breathing is the key to good health, purifying our blood, cleaning our lungs and controlling our entire bodily functions."

Mystic Desmond made these statements:

- Let us all appreciate our Breath because it is our home sweet home! Let us practice breathing consciously, because it is the sweetest thing we can do for ourselves and others.
- Our Breath is the only fountain of eternal youth we are guaranteed to find when we breathe consciously and satisfy our mind.
- Trust your Breath with all your heart, soul and mind simply because it is your sole support!
- If every living cell in our bodies runs on its Breath, can anything in our personal lives be more important than our Breath?
- Our Breath is our truth and substance, our limitless potential and absolute abundance.
- Shallow breathing is the root of all evil, but conscious deep breathing renews and restores the mind, body and soul.
- We are our Breath, Breathing, Pulsating and multiplying ourselves into experiences of light, love and beauty for ourselves and our global family! Come let us celebrate our original sweetness by sweetening our personal and social relationships, one conscious deep breath at a time.

Mystic Desmond closed his presentation by saying; "Before making decisions or facing adversaries, find a quiet place and close your eyes and breathe consciously until you feel your entire body relaxing. Then, listen to every breath you take. Feel every breath you exhale and be aware that no one has the power to upset The Sage Within, without your permission.

Then, make your decisions to face your adversaries with one powerful acknowledgement that you are in control of your internal peace and happiness through your breath.

Your conscious breathing is the master key to empowering The Sage Within."

Every Mystic stood up, and bowed to Mystic Desmond in a sign of appreciation, and spiritually said, thank you Teacher.

After a few minutes of whispering among the Mystics, sharing their comments from the wisdom they received from Mystic Desmond, The Anointed One could not sit quietly anymore and seized the opportunity to follow Mystic Desmond.

When she got to the center of the group, another phase of silence instantly spread through the audience.

She smiled and said, "Breath is all we got! I really appreciate every word of wisdom that Mystic Desmond imparted to us about the power of the breath.

When I look among my fellow Mystics, I see all males except my sister, Sage Chioma.

How many of you while breathing consciously, acknowledged that it was a women's umbilical cord that gave you the breath of life while you were in the womb?"

How many of you are conscious that is was not your father's breath that kept you alive, but the breath of the woman you call mother?

Now that you are reminded of the source (woman) that was breathing for you for approximately nine months until you could breathe on your own, how important of a role that tree of life (woman) should play in your lives?

And don't you think that this 'Tree of Life' is deserving of our unconditional respect and trust?

Both male and female get their oxygen from the same source and we both exhale carbon dioxide."

All of our internal organs are the same except for our sexual organs and breasts."

Nature has given us an abundance of evidence to the equality of us all as human beings.

I overheard a few of you sharing with each other your age.

The average age I heard was between 85 and 117 years old. I am 142 years old."

It seemed like a shock wave went through the group. One Mystic said, "I thought she was about 65 years old. Another said I put her no more than 85 years old."

"My fellow Mystics brothers and sister, I am here to share the secrets to my fountain of youth.

Little did I realize that my youthful looks are due in part to my daily quiet meditation and conscious breathing.

"Now, I have a better understanding of the importance of conscious breathing to my good health.

Thank you Mystic Desmond for sharing with us such profound and undisputable information.

After spending three months in the deep jungle studying animal's eating behavior, we returned to our villages and adopted a complete vegetarian diet."

When we observed the birth of cows, goats, sheep and horses, we noticed that their offspring start walking immediately. Therefore, the quality of the milk that those offspring needs in order to develop fast is not the same milk a human child needs.

We encourage feeding breast milk to all of the newborn in our villages."

"We learned that the human small intestine where the food processing takes place is almost 2,700 square feet long."

"Can you imagine the amount of food that can be stored in a space that is approximately 2,700 square feet?"

"In order to prevent food from decomposing within our bodies or trying to eliminate itself from our bodies in the form of rash, sores or other skin and facial abnormalities, we use special herb teas to help the elimination process."

"There is a tree the medicine doctors of our village discovered and if you eat the leaf or drink it as a tea, it will help to maintain your youthful look. We call that tree of life, Moringa. It is one of the most powerful medicinal plants on planet earth."

"We have another amazing medicinal plant named *Ganja.* We call this plant, the *Village Doctor* because of its long list of medicinal benefits.

The Anointed One said; "I was surprised when a fire broke out in my village and a little child got burned and one of the local medicine doctors poured honey on the burn and it helped to heal it. How many of you know that honey is an antiseptic for burns?

The Aloe plant is another one of my secrets. I use it as a drink. It helps to clean my internal system. It is also perfect for burns, especially the yellow liquid that drips out of a freshly cut aloe plant.

Another important ingredient to good health and a youthful look is the quality of the water you drink.

Make sure you are drinking water in which humans are not swimming or bathing. Make sure that human or animal wastes do not get discharged in the water you drink. I suggest you only drink the water coming from the highest hill in the form of a waterfall.

I was told that if I squeeze a half of lime in my water, it will help to improve the quality of that water. This creates a welcome disease-free balance in the cells.

Here comes the real secret that will allow each one of you to *Die Young at an Old Age* and that is, 'you are what you think!

Your thoughts are the roots that will determine your good health and youthful looks. If you can master your mind, then, you will be the master of The Sage Within."

"If you are doing conscious breathing, eating well, but have negative thoughts and feelings, then, those thoughts and things will show up in the form of lines on your face, body and hands.

Your negative thoughts and emotions are the stimulus to start the human decaying process.

Negative thoughts send a message to your entire body that says, I cannot cope with these issues, they are beyond my control, and therefore, I am ready to checkout from this earthly experience.

Keep up those negative thoughts and watch your body obey your mental command by making your life miserable and by creating pain where none should exist."

Your negative mental state of mind is so powerful, that it will do its best to prepare you for your transition to the other world.

Proper conscious breathing, on the other hand, can help you overcome those negative thoughts.

I recalled on one of my trips to India where I was told by a yogi that the human mind is like a monkey; incessantly active by its own nature. Then it becomes drunk by the wine of desire, thus increasing its turbulence. Desire takes possession; there comes the sting of the scorpion of jealousy of others whose desires meet with greater fulfillment. Last of all, the demon of pride takes possession of the mind, making it think itself of all importance.

How hard it is to control such a mind? It is our responsibility to control that restless, drunk, scorpion bitten, demon possessed mind and to make it do certain things, attend to certain things, while refraining from doing other things and attending to distracting things. *Master your mind and you master your destiny!*

Understanding that you are the master of your destiny is another key you need to exercise.

Acknowledging 'The Sage Within,' tapping into the universal source and quietly communicating with your ancestors for answers, will give you positive results.

You follow those steps and you will '*die young at a very old age.*'

The first woman to address Mystics at any major conference got a standing ovation which ended the negative image of women among the majority of Mystics from all walks of life.

She whispered to her sister and said, "*My dear, many of the Mystics here today will go home and for the first time, see the Divinity in their daughters and wives.*

Many will acknowledge quietly that energy and vibration are not gender bias and since nature is not that way, man should not create an environment that support or legalizes gender biases."

It was getting very late and the group decided to adjourn the event until 7:00 am the following morning.

During their break, The Anointed One and Sage Chioma became very friendly with one of the senior Mystic by the name of Diop. Mystic Diop was very fascinated with the sisters' energy and vibration and shared his vision for them.

His advice was for them to continue on their path and to do their best in understanding nature's magnetic fields. He said that anyone who mastered and understood the migration of animals, especially during reproductive periods, will open one of nature's secrets with unlimited possibilities.

The sisters tried to sleep that night, but the information shared with them by Mystic Diop was so profound and prophetic, they stayed up in search of answers.

5:00 a.m. that morning, everyone was taking a bath under one of nature's picturesque waterfalls. There was also a small lake with bubbling hot water coming from Mother Earth. It was amazing to see the cold waterfall next to the heated bubbling natural pool. It is as though Mother Nature was showing us the use of hot & cold water to enhance good health.

At 7:00 am, the group was seated and ready to resume the event.

From the extreme back of the group, a well groomed young man walked up to the front and introduced himself.

"My fellow Mystics, brothers and sisters, my name is Mystic Baratunde better known as the Food Alchemist. I was never interested in learning how to convert metal into gold. My focus is how to convert food into nutritional medicine for the mind, body and soul.

I was exposed to the Chinese Ying and Yang philosophy.

The Chinese word for energy is known as (Chee). In order for ying and yang to be balanced and for the body to be healthy, Qi (Chee) must be balanced and flowing freely.

I learned all about The Forgotten Foods from Ancient bygone Mystics. My tonics are meticulously processed by hand, aged and buried on a new moon for months in the earth, for a natural electro-magnetic harmonization and unearthed on a full moon."

"They are charged again with a family of Amethyst crystals and with Qi Kung energy and only then…ready for use.

No product comes to our family until it is aged for at least 13 moons. This one-of-a-kind unique alchemical process gives our finished products a high frequency vibration. Within a flash of a second, Mystic Baratunde turned into Mystic Diop and the entire group screamed in harmony, The Mysticmorphosist!

The old Mystic Diop turned instantly back into Baratunde and said, yes, I am the Master Mysticmorphosist.

Not only did I learn and mastered the Chinese Ying and Yang way of life, I am able to communicate individually with my internal cells. I can turn on and off any cells within my body by sending mentally the proper levels of energy and vibration to any area of my body.

I have walked and participated in many of your lives with a different name and look; I will continue to do so because, when the student is ready, the teacher will materialize.

I am both Mystic Baratunde and Mystic Diop. I am also the Mystic who invisibly influenced your decision to invite The Anointed One and Sage Chioma.

The presence of the two sister Sages makes this the perfect Ying and Yang gathering. It will give each one of us the balance that should be in all gatherings and that is, the energy of both male and female."

He then turned himself into the most beautiful pair of male and female Eagles and flew away.

The group was in total shock. Conversations among small groups took up the rest of the day and by the time they realized that no one else spoke, the event came to an end.

Chioma turned to her sister on the way home and said, "We all are leaving with one understanding and that is, ***There Is a Mysticmorphosist in Everyone One of Us.*** When we master our mind, we master all possibilities…"

Chapter 12

The Anointed One was in a trance while her sister Chioma was sharing those prophetic observations with her. She whispered to Chioma and said, "I am still recovering from the fact that I met and witnessed the creative God within, The Mysticmorphosist. Chioma, only a person with a Cosmic Consciousness can attain such status."

- ## *What Is Cosmic Consciousness?*

Chioma said, "My understanding of Cosmic Consciousness is when we all accept the indisputable fact that all the elements within our body are the same that exist in the Cosmos. When we understand the Laws of the Cosmos, then, we can apply those laws to everything we do in order to be in harmony with the Universe."

The Anointed One then said, "The unlimited world of possibilities becomes a reality when we play by the Cosmic Rule of Law! Yes, that is what the Mysticmorphosist was sharing with us in parables.

Everything is connected. Our thoughts are connected to the oxygen we inhale. The plant kingdom that gives us the breath of life (oxygen) gets its energy and nutrient from the Sun and the water from above and below.

We eat fruits and vegetables from the plants that got their nutrients from Mother Earth. It is obvious that if the earth is composed of oxygen, silicon, aluminum, calcium, potassium and magnesium, then, there are common elements between the earth and us since we have those same elements within."

65

"Based on that fact, we should be able to communicate with each other."

The purity of the fruits and plants we eat are important to keeping the quality of those same elements within our body, and that is one of the keys to Cosmic Consciousness.

This conversation we are having sister, is allowing me to understand what true Cosmic Consciousness is and how we apply those principles to our daily lives. I am now convinced that the quality of the water we drink can have a positive or negative effect on our health because we are about 75 percent water.

We all must become good stewards of Mother Earth. We must be environmentally conscious just to ensure our good health and longevity on planet earth."

The Anointed One interjected by saying, "You are correct. Do you recall when the Mysticmorphosist stated that his medicinal food is aged and buried on a new moon for months in the earth, for a natural electro-magnetic harmonization and then un-earthed on a full moon?

Baratunde-Diop plans and lives his life based on Cosmic Consciousness, which gave him the ability and possibilities to have the power of the creative Cosmic Mind at his disposal. Anyone can control and manipulate this physical body, once they have tapped into the Cosmic Mind's secret codes of the Laws of Nature."

Chioma said; "What I love about the Cosmic Consciousness Laws is that those laws are impartial.

They apply equally to everyone. They work without prejudice. They are not racial or gender biased."

Chapter 13

The Anointed One said to her Sister Chioma that over the years, they had been sharing their knowledge, wisdom and understanding about the Laws of The Universe with other Mystics and Sages and it was now time to share the Mystic Key to Success with everyone so that they can awaken The Sage Within themselves.

• *Awakening The Sage Within*

The two sisters sent out a call to the Mystics and Sages of the world to come together and share their knowledge, wisdom and experiences with people from all walks of life.

The ultimate goal was to raise the positive energy and vibration of the world by empowering each person with the proper secret code that will unlock The Sage Within.

"Once a person is enlightened, they will play an active role in creating peace and tolerance around the world," said Sage Chioma.

"They will become a voice for good health and responsible stewards of the environment.

They will spread the concept of vegetarianism and they each will work towards living in harmony with the Laws of The Universe.

Please pack your bags and come with us on this trip to the holy land of Mystic teachers sharing with the masses, the Mystic Key to Wisdom, Wellness, Happiness, Peace, Longevity and Good Environmental Stewardship."

"You have reached your destination. You have blended with the visitors from around the world, ready to listen and learn the Mystic Codes to unlocking The Sage Within."

There is an instant silence that is spreading rapidly among the various groups and they all are now focused on the center stage where The Anointed One is about to speak.

"It seems like everyone was consciously breathing because you cannot hear one distracting sound, this is what we call a spiritual silent moment.

I would like to welcome everyone, especially those Mystics traveling from afar.

After the event, each Mystic will be available to have small group discussions where questions can be asked.

She asked everyone to remember these words:

'Every earthly and cosmic element will reveal its Secrets to you if you approach it with love, sincerity and a protective spirit.'

Before I share some of my Mystic Secrets with you, please remember also that hearing is one of our five senses, but *Listening* is a skill that you must master before you can awaken The Sage Within.

When you master the art of listening, it allows your ears to hear the message with a focused and receptive mind.

Each one of us cannot change our parents or the year we were born, but we have the choice to select our clothing and friends. Make sure they both fit you perfectly."

"Now that you are no longer hearing me, but listening with a focused and receptive mind, you are all ready to receive the Mystic Keys to Wisdom, Wellness, Happiness, Peace, Longevity and Good Environmental Stewardship.

The real secret is that there are No secrets to reveal to you.'

What we are about to share is a way of life that will allow you to live in harmony with God's Laws of Nature. We suffer when we violate those laws consciously or unconsciously."

- **Mystic Secret Key # 1**

The Anointed One said: "Whenever anyone asks you where you do live? It is important to respond that you live 24/7 in your body and sometimes you stay at XYZ address, village or country. It's your duty to spread the consciousness that we all live within our bodies.

Whoever you say those words to, that person will repeat them to others and this consciousness of living 24/7 in our bodies will spread like wildfire.

Once this acknowledgement becomes part of our lives, it will be communicated in the villages, at home, to our children and among strangers.

The Sage Within will now become concerned and protective of what we put inside of our home (body) not where we sometimes stay physically.

Such knowledge will shift our focus from desiring more beautiful clothes to put on our body at the expense of our internal peace and good health."

"Investing in the most beautiful earthly home by compromising the quality of our internal permanent home will be something of the past.

Once you reach such a level of enlightenment, you will become protective of your environment. Any action that affects your environment or food production is going to affect the quality of water or food that you put inside your internal temple.

An Enlightened Sage knows that he or she can change his or her external perceptions, but cannot change the fact that they live 24/7 within their bodies. Therefore, The Sage Within will take the necessary steps to have a clean, healthy and comfortable home."

The Anointed One shared a powerful secret when she said, "I was able to empower and raise the level of consciousness of The Sage Within me, by acknowledging that I should be very protective of how I interpret things I hear and see because, my eyes and ears are doorways to my 24/7 internal home.

What I believe lives within me and affects my emotional state of happiness.

Hatred, jealousy and revenge have no room in the house of an Enlightened Sage Within."

At that point, The Anointed One asked Mystic Dyer to come up and share his thoughts on the subject at hand.

Mystic Dyer asked, "If you squeezed an orange what will come out of it?" And the answer was, "orange juice."

He then asked "why orange juice?" And the common answer he got was, "Because that is what is inside of it."

Dyer continued "When someone challenges you (squeezes you) or upsets you and your response is anger, revenge, hatred, then, you need to understand that is what is inside of you.

The Sage Within will never be awakened as long as you allow such elements like anger, revenge and hatred to occupy space within your internal temple.

The Sage Within will hide itself until it feels that it is safe to come out and occupy your temple of inner peace without the presence of negative elements.

You are what you think; therefore, your thoughts are very powerful. For example, if I tell you not to think of a coconut, you immediately vision one. You just cannot stop the brain from working. What you need to do is to replace negative and unwelcomed thoughts with positive and digestible images.

The thing that stimulates The Sage Within to wake up is a pleasant and peaceful internal living environment that is in harmony with God's Universal Laws."

Mystic Dyer said, "The world we live in is of our own mental creation. We can change our world by changing our thoughts.

Each one of us traveled a long distance to be here in search of knowledge.

We should acknowledge that all the changes must take place internally. So, we can awaken The Sage Within regardless where our physical bodies are presently located.

We have a list of distinguished Mystics ready to share their Mystic Secret Keys with you. Let me close by making this statement."

"Before you can be the Master of your destiny and allow The Sage Within to perform all the great miracles of life on your behalf, the Sage must be awakened and we have given you the basic key you need to perform in order to awaken The Sage Within.

Purge your soul of all anger, revenge, hatred or jealousy and watch the enlightened Sage Within transform your internal chaotic home into your Temple of Inner Peace."

Mystic Dyer asked the group to, "Close your eyes, breathe consciously and purge your minds of all negative thoughts and emotions. Forgive all those who have hurt you and ask the universe to forgive you for all the hurt and pain you have caused others."

Mystic Dyer explained, "Since we live with ourselves 24/7, we must be good tenants by keeping our environment clean and peaceful. Our physical presence on planet earth is a gift from the Creator and as such, we should do our best to keep our internal environment spiritually in harmony with God's Universal Laws."

Each person listened to the words of wisdom spoken by Mystic Dyer. They continued their meditation for hours without realizing the passage of time.

Each one was in search of their elusive Sage Within and was doing everything necessary to create the right environment to stimulate the Sage to come out from its restful state.

After hours of meditation, everyone opened their eyes and shared with each other their journey. Their mannerisms were more subtle and peaceful. Everybody could see a change in the atmosphere.

There was no doubt that many of them were able to awaken The Sage Within, while others were able to at least stimulate The Sage Within. A metamorphosis to Sagehood was taking place.

- **Mystic Secret Key # 2**

After hours of reflection from the mental and spiritual journey they had taken, all were ready for the next Mystic Secret Key.

At the center of the group, we are seeing for the first time an Ancient Gong. The Anointed One walked up to the gong and gave it one bang that sent a spiritual vibratory rippling sound that got everyone's attention. The group gathered and was ready for the next Mystic messenger.

Mystic Zakutee standing next to The Anointed One, opened by saying, *now that you have awakened The Sage Within, we need to understand the environment where The Sage lives 24/7.*

"Once you understand all the elements of The Sage Within, then, and only then, can you become the master of your own destiny. What I am about to share with you is information you need in order to make wise decisions, instead of leaving your destiny into the hands of others."

Mystic Zakutee invited everyone to come with him on a historical search to find all the elements within our bodies that also exist on earth and in the far galaxies of the universe.

We are about to see the truth that we are connected to everything that we can view with our naked eyes and also those that elude our physical vision.

"Each human has the following elements within: *Oxygen, Hydrogen, Nitrogen, Calcium, Magnesium, Phosphorus, Sulfur, Iron, Zinc, Borox, Iodine, Potassium, Lead, Copper, Manganese, Selenium and Fluorine.*

Through our relationship with well-known Master Mystic Alchemists, we learned that the ***Air* has the following elements**:

Nitrogen, Oxygen, Argon, Carbon Dioxide, Neon, Methane, Helium, Krypton, Hydrogen, Xenon, Ozone, Nitrogen Dioxide, Iodine, Carbon Monoxide, and Ammonia."

You can now understand why the quality of the air we breathe is important to the good health of The Sage Within?

Here are the elements of the Sun. Please observe how many of those elements are within each one of us: *Hydrogen, Helium, Oxygen, Carbon, Nitrogen, Silicon, Magnesium, Neon, Iron, and Sulfur."*

Mystic Zakutee said that he wanted to know **the elements within the crust of the earth** since that's where the roots of the trees that bear fruits which we eat are located.

"I found a Master Earth Alchemist who gave me the elements within the crust of Mother Earth. Here is a birds-eye-view of the list: *Oxygen, Silicon, Aluminum, Iron, Calcium, Sodium, Potassium, Magnesium, Titanium, Hydrogen, Phosphorus, Manganese, Fluorine, Barium, Carbon, Strontium, Sulfur, Zirconium, Tungsten, Vanadium, Chlorine, Rubidium, Chromium, Copper, Nitrogen, Nickel and Zinc."*

Mystic Zakutee got the attention of everyone when he said, "***All humans are conscious of inhaling every second air/oxygen,*** but only *Mystics and Sages are conscious of inhaling all the elements of air."*

"The Mystic Secret Key in Step #2 teaches you the various elements that exist within us and our environment and its relationship and inter-connectivity to the cosmic world, which is a rite of passage to entering Sagehood.

Can you imagine how each one of us could be in control of our internal world, if we could have every element within our bodies communicating with its counterpart within the earth, in the air, the sun and the galaxy?

You might say that is impossible. You also would have said that since a butterfly's body is heavier that its wings, it should not be able to fly, but it flies!

I have witnessed people suffering from various illnesses who were cured by giving them a daily dose of Sun exposure (Sun bath) which is the greatest source of Vitamin D.

Now that you understand the role of the Sun in the production of Vitamin D, you will welcome the Sun every morning by sitting and absorbing its rays for at least one hour, while those uninitiated into Sagehood will run for cover. *The darker (melanin) skin complexion, the more sun is needed to generate the proper daily level of Vitamin D."*
As The Anointed One mentioned before, even though we are listening to the various Mystic Secret Keys, there are no Secret Codes. All we are doing is sharing a way of life that is practiced by those we call Mystics and Sages."

Once you study the elements that exist within you and compare those with the elements of the Water you drink, the Air you inhale, and the Sun, whose rays affect both you as a person, stimulates the photosynthesis in plants, you can then make better decisions that are in harmony with the Laws of the Universe.

Mystics and Sages understand very well that heat from the Sun causes water to evaporate from the surface of lakes, rivers and oceans into water vapor in the atmosphere.

We Mystics also know that plants, after absorbing water from the ground, "sweat" water vapor through their leaves to stay cool. These plant sweating processes help to get water into the atmosphere. Ancient Alchemists call this process *transpiration!*

This is why we Mystics and Sages are active environmental stewards, because we know that the quality of the water that is being evaporated, will determine the cleanliness of the rainwater that will come back down to earth and nourish our plants. It also determines the purity of the water we drink and the standard of the water we use to bathe.

One of the things Mystics learn is that our skin is our largest organ and through it pores, external elements are absorbed and therefore, even the purity of the water that touches our skin is of concern to Mystics."

Mystic Zakutee stated that it is important to understand why Mystics and Sages walk on Mother Earth barefooted.

Indigenous people from all walks of life have done this throughout the ages. Their secret is now revealed… underneath the bottom of the human feet are pressure points and meridians that are stimulated with every barefoot step you take.

With this awareness, you will now be more likely to add 'Earth Grounding' to your Sun Bath, creating a 'Sun and Earth Grounding ritual.'

Yes, you will intensify the electro-magnetic frequency coming up into your feet and distributed throughout your body each day during your Earth Bath."

Now you understand why washing of the feet is an honor.

After traversing the earth, a weary Sage would appreciate the honor of having a footbath, which allows the giver and receiver to exchange blessings further stimulating the pressure points, regulating and harmonizing the body."

"This brings to mind the physical, emotional and psychological benefits of hugging" said Mystic Zakutee.

"Hugs boost oxytocin levels, which heal feelings of isolation, anger and loneliness. It releases tension and can take away pain. Hugs strengthen and stymulate our internal doctor (defense system).

The nurturing touch of a hug builds trust and a sense of security. Hugging relaxes muscles and teaches us how to give and receive."

Mystic Zakutee stated, "There are many cultures where men do not hug other men and in those cultures, the trust level is very low among men.

The relationship between fathers and sons are not as close as the relationship in cultures where father and sons hug on a daily basis."

Mystic Zakutee pointed out, "The reason why we must incorporate laughter into our daily spiritual diet is because people who have a belly-full of laughter before bed, sleep better.

Laughter stretches muscles in our face and body. It raises our blood pressure and makes us breathe faster, sending more oxygen to our tissues. Laughter also improves alertness, creativity and memory."

He closed by saying, "This is why Hugging & Laughter are two of the main healing characteristics of An Enlightened Sage."

- **Mystic Secret Key # 3**

The Anointed One, walked to the Gong, gave it another bang, announcing the readiness of the next Mystic to speak.

After gathering, they were ready for the message from another Mystic. The entire group was in awe of the six foot gorgeous 45 year old woman from the Watusi tribe standing next to The Anointed One.

The Anointed One introduced Mystic Habimana by saying, "I am proud to introduce you to our next presenter. Her name is Habimana and many of you know that's a Watusi male name."

I was responsible for naming her. I encouraged her parents to balance her being by giving her a male name. This should open doors for her where women are not allowed.

She is a protégé of both Sage Chioma and I and there is no doubt she has a lot to share with you on how to awaken The Sage Within.

Mystic Habimana stood in front of the group and for about three minutes, she said nothing. To the onlookers, it seemed like hours.

Then, she broke her silence by saying, "When you speak, punctuate with pause (silent moments) and when you have nothing to say, say nothing. Embracing those silent meditative moments is the 3rd Mystic Key in the awakening of The Sage Within."

Soft Spoken Mystic Habimana said, "Even though we are interactive beings, having silent space between an active engagement and self-reflection, is important to our internal growth. We Mystics use our communication skills to share with the world what we know and we take the silent moments to reflect on what we said."

"Those silent moments between engagement and self-reflection, is the space we use to get inspiration and spiritual enlightenment from our ancestors and the Cosmic Mind."

Mystic Habimana expounded by saying, "That true spiritual silence is freedom and the absence of oneself.

True silence is blank. There is no vision or objects, just empty space. You should be able to hear your heartbeat, the blood flowing through your veins, while in a state of weightlessness and nonexistence.

From the time we wake up until we go to bed, the majority of us are faced with external noise. Before rising each morning, take a few minutes to clear your mind and listen to your breath.

When there is silence, there is time for introspection and to allow your true self to awaken."

Mystic Habimana told the group, "All Mystics will find themselves in situations where others disagree with their ideology or way of life. You can subdue aggression while keeping your energy by simply looking at the aggressor, while saying absolutely nothing.

When others are speaking, silence is a respectful and proper behavior to adopt. Please note what we all learned about the difference between hearing and listening.

A True Mystic combines the power of silence with the supremacy of listening in order to understand clearly what is being said.

Body language is another great communication medium: therefore, use your facial expressions and physical movements to acknowledge that you are listening.

Mystics seldom disagree with the views of others; instead, they will ask the person to please expand on their statement or belief for better understanding. Mystics are always in search of understanding.

Master Mystics accept this truth: perfect ideas or thoughts only exist in our minds. The minute we implement these ideas or share those thoughts with others, they are now subject to acceptance or criticism, therefore, accepting and dealing with criticism is part of our daily lives. It is another basic principle of true Mystics."

Mystic Habimana told the group: "Always remember that words are powerful, because, our interpretation of spoken words can cause happiness or sadness. That is why silence sometimes is an appropriate answer."

"Our body gestures, facial expressions, posture and eye movements, sometimes speak louder than words," said Mystic Habimana.

She continued by saying: "That is why Mystics adopt a neutral, unemotional body posture during conversations, especially during listening moments. They want you to listen to their words, not interpret their body language."

Mystic Habimana closed her message by asking everyone to "Close your eyes and take a mental journey to a world of unlimited empty space. Enjoy the conscious silent, weightless, floating moments of the mind.

Be at peace with yourself and the living universe. Stays in that space as long as you want, then, quietly return to this place and time. You will then return home feeling relaxed and rejuvenated."

- **Mystic Secret Key # 4**

The Anointed One, walked up to the Gong, gave it another bang to get the attention of everyone, signaling once more, the presence of another Mystic messenger.

Mystic Mahavani of India was introduced as the voice of reasoning. He opened his message by asking, "How many of you believe and accept the fact that knowledge is power?" Every hand went up and he then said, "Each one of you is wrong."

"Knowledge is not power, only applied knowledge is power. What you learned here is knowledge, but if you never practice it, then, it is wasted!"

Mystics from all walks of life are great listeners because they each learned one fundamental fact and that is, you can only get knowledge from personal experience.

If you do not have firsthand experience of something that happened, then, it becomes information, not knowledge.

We listen to individuals who claim to have knowledge of things that happened 200 to 500 years ago based on information that was passed down through generations.

If you did not witness what you are speaking about, then, you have no firsthand knowledge.

We can have strong belief and we take a stand on an issue because we believe the information we have received is true, even though we have no personal knowledge that it is true.

When you awaken The Sage Within, you are at the same time activating your internal reasoning and logical thinking process. You become more cautious of what you claim to be the gospel truth.

An Enlightened Sage uses terms like, "Based on the information I was given' or 'based on what I have read, I believe this to be true,' instead of saying, 'I know this to be factual or truthful,' even though you cannot defend what you believe based on personal knowledge."

Mystic Mahavani told the group: "When you master the art of listening, only then, are you able to distinguish conversations that are based on knowledge and information masquerading as knowledge."

"Mystic Mahavani spoke about religion as a very sensitive area that we must be very cautious about when we find ourselves in the center of a spiritual debate.

All religious beliefs are based on information that we learned from writings or rituals handed down through generations," said Mystic Mahavani.

We were not personally present when those religious words or statements were made; therefore, we have no true and personal knowledge about the doctrine on which we based our religious beliefs, even though we strongly believe in those words we say are pious.

It is sad when someone is killed or banned from a village or family due to the fact that person's religious belief is not the same as those of the village or family."

Mystic Mahavani recalled during his early training when he asked an Ancient Mystic Dali Lama what is the best religion and he said: *"The best religion is that one that gets you closer to God. It is the one that makes you a better person."*

"Whatever makes you more compassionate, more sensible, more loving, more humanitarian, more responsive and more ethical, the religion that will do that for you, is the best religion"

The most powerful words I learned that day from the Ancient Mystic Dali Lama, was when he said to me:

"Take care of your Thoughts because they become your Words. Take care of your Words because they become your Actions. Take care of your Actions because they become your Habits. Take care of your Habits because they become your Character."

"I just shared my knowledge of what was said to me by the Mystic, Ancient Dali Lama."

"You now have that *information* and even though you might share such wonderful words of caution with others by saying that those are the words of an Ancient Mystic Dali Lama, you have no personal knowledge that those words were truly given to me by the Ancient Mystic Dali Lama."

"When we master the difference between Knowledge and Information, we become less of a critic and more trustworthy. Tolerance of others ideology and philosophy of life, plays a major part of a Mystic's life.

If you become upset or reject those who hold opposite views from yours, then, you should be disappointed with yourself, because your views today are certainly different from those you had 5, 10 or 15 years ago.

Mystics are tolerant of the views of others, their ideology and philosophy, but they will not participate in any environment that deprives others of their freedom. Mystics reject anything that separate anyone based on racial, social, gender or spiritual ideology.

Please note another truth on your journey to becoming a Sage. There is no school or training that can endorse you as a true Sage. Becoming a Sage is a way of life and you will know when you arrive.

The greatest endorsement you can get is when the world acknowledges and recognizes The Sage Within you.

Mystic Mahavani closed by saying, "Once you master Sagehood, then you will understand the power of *The Laws of Attraction*."

The gathering came to an end for that day, with individuals assembled in groups who shared with each other what they learned.

Based on the various interactions, it seems like it was a tasteful and digestible full plate of food for thought they all received. Their mental appetite was craving for more…

- **Mystic Secret Key # 5**

Sage Chioma walked towards the center of the group and for the first time, gave the Gong a bang, but this time, for some reason, it was not as loud as before; it had a melodic tone that got everyone's attention.

Mystic Walkerini was introduced as the messenger of the Laws of Attraction.

He then proceeded to address the group by saying, "You are about to understand the real truth behind *The Laws of Attraction*.

There is a term that you must clearly remember and it is called, Universal Truth. Universal truth speaks about an action that will repeat itself over and over again without failure.

Oxygen is a universal truth. It's the same oxygen we breathe regardless where on planet earth we are standing.

The Sun is another universal truth. It will rise regardless if the clouds are blocking it or not."

"The common interpretation of The Law of Attraction says that you attract into your life whatever you think about. Your dominant thoughts will find a way to manifest."

A Mystic will ask, "Is there a universal truth to the above statement? After a moment of silence, he might come up with the following answers, "Yes and No.

There is truth that your dominant thoughts will find a way to manifest itself. Here is an ancient mystic story that will give clarity to the statement."

A wise Indian Mystic took his grandson to the top of the highest mountain and from that point it seemed that they could just extend their hands and touch the sky. He then sat him down to teach him the ways of life."

The Indian Mystic turned to his grandson and said, "A fight is going on inside me," he told the young boy, "A terrible fight between two wolves.

One is evil, full of anger, sorrow, regret, greed, self-pity and false pride. The other is good, full of joy, peace, love, humility, kindness, forgiveness and faith.

This same fight is going on inside of you, grandson…and inside of every other person on this earth. The grandson ponders this for a moment and then asks, "Grandfather, which wolf will win?"

The Ancient Indian Mystic smiled and simply said, "***The One You Feed The Most***. Whichever thought you give energy to, will become the dominant one and will consume you for better or worse."

"Based on the philosophy behind the Law of Attraction, we Mystics strongly agree with it as it relates to one's internal thoughts and results. You create your world based on your own thoughts or interpretations of what you see or hear.

You have total control of your happiness or sadness based on your own thoughts and beliefs. There is no external force that can influence your state of mind without your permission. You own the master lock to The Sage Within."

Mystic Walkerini continued by saying, "Now let us look at the Laws of Attraction as it relates to external forces."

"The common interpretation of the Laws of Attraction says that you attract into your life whatever you think about. Can we say with certainty that whatever we think about can have a direct effect good or bad on the Laws of The Universe?

We Mystics have reached the conclusion that once we understand the Laws of The Universe; those principles can be applied within our daily lives in order to be in harmony with nature and ourselves.

To say that our thoughts can influence and change the Laws of Nature, violates everything we have been taught about The Creator's Code of Nature. For example, the code for creating a child is applicable universally; it cannot be mentally manipulated by any human being.

Mystics believe that man basically is always in search of happiness and each person has the same amount of energy and vibration.

If one person decides to be revengeful or destructive and burns down a village one night, those good souls who lost their lives and those suffering from serious burns, can we say they attracted such a vicious act upon themselves?

Because we live in a world where man has free-will, we will come in contact with people from all walks of life, beliefs, ideologies, philosophies and spirituality exercising their feel will.

Based on the above, do you think that we can truly influence others as a result of our thoughts or passions?

Do we really attract into our lives whatever we think about or do we attract based on our actions, behavior, and reputation…good or bad?

We learned earlier that knowledge is not power; only applied knowledge is power. Can we say the same for our thoughts as it relates to external desires? That they only exist in our head until we decide to implement them?

The passion we possess for a particular idea manifests itself through our mannerism, our attitude, or our body expression when we speak about our project and this is what attracts others to us.

As an aspiring Sage, it must be clear in your mind that you are not attracting physical things into your life. You are acknowledging individuals of like minds who will facilitate you in getting the things you want in life.

Since we at this time have not reached the level where we can read each other's minds, we get to know each other based on verbal communication and through others whom we have shared our passion and they in turn, impart our philosophy to others who then will seek us out."

"We must be careful how we use the term, The Law of Attraction.

If we are mentally focused with a passion to have the largest home in a village, what does that mean?

In order to get that home, we must cut down some trees in order to get the lumber we need to build it. By cutting down trees, there is a great possibility that we might disrupt the habitat of animals and insects that occupied that space for thousands of years in violation of the Laws of Nature.

By removing trees, we are reducing the capacity of that area to absorb carbon dioxide in violation of the Laws of Nature.

Then, the question we must ask when we speak about The Laws of Attraction is this, are the things we mentally desire is in harmony with The Laws of Nature?

The more we humans evolve and our wants and desires increases, we expand our territorial ownership by forcing animals and insects who occupied those lands for millions of years, further into the forest and many into extinction.

Based on our teeth structure, we were made to grind our food. There is no digestive system within humans to digest raw meat. Our mental desire for animal meat has many of us killing even the closest animal to man for consumption, the Gorillas.

I would like to repeat one important point for you to better understand The Laws of Attraction. There is truth to the statement that we attract everything into our lives, the good and the bad.

"What is not explained within that truth is, if we must socialize with other fellow human beings, we automatically will come in contact with good and bad people.

At least once in our lives, we will be present when bad and good things happen and we might be the victims of some of those bad events, because it so happened that we were there when it occurred."

"Sages are very analytical. They try to separate fact from fiction," said Mystic Walkerini.

"What distinguishes a Sage from others," he asked? He answered by saying, "Sages always try to adopt a solution that is non-confrontational and at the same time, the solution must be in harmony with The Laws of Nature."

Sages put human life and happiness before material wealth.

Mystics strongly feel that it is not the amount of breath that we take during a lifetime that really matter, it is the moments that take our breath away, that really matter.

That is why Sages can spend hours sitting next to a waterfall or near a river listening to the music of nature. It is why Sages stare at the moonlit sky and enjoy Mother Nature's celestial theatre.

The Law of Attraction therefore has two sides. The Internal Law of Attractions of which you are definitely in control. Whatever you think will have a direct effect on you mentally, physically and spiritually.

The external Law of Attraction deals with your interaction with the outside world."

"You usually have no control of this side since, you are only one of the actors or participants exercising his or her Free Will.

Mystics define Free Will as each person's freedom to make choices without the interference of any deity."

Mystic Walkerini said, "If we claim that God does bless people daily, then we are saying that man does not have Free Will because it can be interrupted by God at any time.

Without metaphysical freedom, the universe is just a divine puppet show.

If you truly agree that God's Laws (codes) of Nature are working 24/7 and if man violates any of those codes while exercising his or her Free will, then, the violator or violators will experience punishment based on the violation. *The Laws of Attraction cannot influence mentally The Laws of Nature. The Law of Attraction must work in harmony with God's Laws of Nature, not influence it at will.*

For example, if pure water is one of the main pillars for good health and longevity and man violates our water system by polluting it, then, man will suffer health problems because he violated one of God's Laws of Nature.

Based on the above, we all learned that man can exercise his Free Will by adhering to the Laws of Nature or be in violation of those codes which carry deadly human and environmental penalties.

You can better understand the external Laws of Attraction when you clearly agree that if a group of individuals pollute a body of water, that pollution will affect not only the violators, but every individual who comes in contact with that polluted body of water."

"Can we honestly say that those innocent victims attracted whatever bad health they are now experiencing due to a few violators? This we call Negative Uncontrollable External Attraction."

Mystic Walkerini asked the group, "Think about this one question, do you believe that villagers all exercising their Free Will can attract exactly what they are thinking about at a given moment in time?"

Can those who want rain for their farms and on the same day and time, another group wants sun because of a major activity taking place in the village; can each have their wishes fulfilled at the same time? How can a group of individuals exercising their Free Will by manipulating The Laws of Nature to their advantage?

Mystic Walkerini closed by quoting the Ancient Mystic Paine: *"The word of the Creator (whoever you conceive the Creator to be,) is the Creation we behold and it is this word, which no human invention can counterfeit or alter, that The Creator speaks universally to man."*

"Even though we have certain control over our internal world based on the way we think, The Laws of Attraction cannot alter the External Laws (Codes) of Creation by focusing on a dominant thought with passion."

Mystic Walkerini continued his closing remarks by reminding each one, "You have witnessed the Mysticmorphosist changing his appearance from Mystic Diop to Mystic Baratunde, because he is in total control of his thoughts and everything within his internal world.

"I know how hard the Mysticmorphosist tried to manipulate his external world by using the power of thinking and visual imagination on many occasions without success.

Each one of you might be asking the same question, "How do I know that The Mysticmorphosist tried to use the external Laws of Attraction without success?"

"Well, I am not only Mystic Walkerini, I am also the Mysticmorphosist. He immediately changed himself into Mystic Baratunde, then to Mystic Diop and back to Mystic Walkerini."

He walked off after saying these prophetic words: "Maybe one day, one of you might tap into the secret codes of The Sage Within that opens the possibility of you mastering the external Laws of Attraction."

Closing Gathering

After two days of relaxation and sharing of experiences, the Gong was banged for the last time; all the Mystics gathered to collectively share their spiritual evolution and to give prophetic guidance to all attending who are in search of The Sage Within.

There were three women among the Mystics on stage and approximately 35% of the attendees were women, on their path to becoming Sages.

The natives made sure that each person present had fresh coconut water which they claimed is the favorite drink of The Sage Within. They said that, "When you close your eyes while drinking coconut water, your entire body goes into a spiritual state of enlightenment. You feel weightless and enter a state of peacefulness."

The silence was broken when Mystic Walkerini opened by saying, "I am the Mysticmorphosist who is also known to many of you as Mystic Baratunde and Mystic Diop. When I take on the personality of any of the mentioned Mystics, I become them in their entirety. For example, when I am Mystic Baratunde, I am one hundred percent the Food Alchemist."

"What each one of you is not aware of, is that you too, perform daily acts of metamorphosis.

I am seeing you today as a person in search of The Sage Within, but there is no doubt that on a daily basis; you transform yourself into a father, mother, farmer, religious leader, village doctor, a son, or a daughter.

Each time you transform yourself mentally and emotionally into any of the above-mentioned characters, they must be in harmony with all your other personalities and that is where it becomes important to master The Sage Within.

You must find that harmonious balance between your spiritual world and the earthly planet you are presently occupying. This is true harmony in mind, body and soul.

You should never spend too much time within the spiritual world by abandoning your planetary presence because you live 24/7 within your temporal temple.

You will have developed the perfect balance between your spiritual and material world when you reach the *I Am Consciousness* stage."

Sage Chioma spoke by saying, "When you reach Sagehood you will know. You would have completely eliminated words that hurt. Complaints and lies will no longer be part of your vocabulary and you would be completely receptive to criticism, unkind words and verbal challenges without it affecting your temple of inner peace.

When you speak, your tone will not give the impression that "*I am more enlightened than you*" instead, "*You acknowledge the divinity in those you meet.*"

Mystic Tikimotu, who never spoke before said, "If you have a choice to be right or to be kind during a debate or discussion, be kind."

Mystic Tikimotu remembered when he was being trained in the art of Aikido, his instructor told him, "*I am teaching you the art of how to suppress aggression, not how to destroy the aggressor.*

Kind words are the suppressors of aggression. Be conscious of others needs and complaints, by not only hearing what they are saying, but responsively listening to every word they are speaking."

Mystic Mokito said in a passionate way, "Be careful of religious debates. Always remember that religious tolerance should be a permanent part of The Sage Within.

All the Ancient religions, preachers, philosophers, village doctors, fortune tellers and all other spiritualists are all seeking the same answers:

* Why are we here?
* Who created us?
* What is beyond death?
* Who created the galaxy?
* Are there other lives in the Universe?"

Judge no person based on their religious persuasion, race, place of birth or gender."

Mystic Mokito reminded the group that one of the most powerful tools The Sage Within has to use to suppress aggression is sincere and honest kind words.

The Anointed One broke her silence by saying, "Look around and let us acknowledge the breathless mountains that border us."

"Have you noticed the musical birds singing all day to us? Are you listening to the ocean waves creating its mystical music? Are you now aware of The Sage Within, ready to be awakened?

"If your answer is yes, then, you have witnessed the Creator in all its manifestations."

There was an instant change in the Anointed One's mood when she said, "I am not sure that a 1,000 years ago, our ancestors would have imagined how much humans would evolve mentally and spiritually."

Today, instead of us fearing the unknown like our ancestors did, we are becoming more curious and willing to explore it.

Based on the above observation, what would each one of you think this world would be like 5,000 years from now?

I am here teaching you how to live longer and healthier and by assisting you to live longer; I am helping to shape the future.

The Anointed One explained, "If we are now living longer, there will be more people on planet earth 5,000 years from now.

With more people living, we have to cut down more trees to build homes for them. This act alone is going to have a negative effect on animals, birds, insect habitats and the environment.

With people living longer, I can see the increase in fishing, hunting and farming. This is going to create a major war between humans and nature. Humans will want to expand their territorial ownership and that act also is going to make nature vulnerable to many catastrophes."

"With humans living longer, 5,000 years from now, some type of teaching or control has to be developed in order to keep track of what each person actions?

I can imagine 5,000 years from now, how man might be fighting with each other to protect and control the limited food supplies around the world.

Those who understand that we cannot increase the amount of land on earth, can only imagine what future humans are going to do, to share equally the limited amount of land to a very large group of humans who are working hard to *Die Young At a Very Old Age*.

We are concerned about how this present generation is dumping our human waste into the rivers and oceans. What will happen if a thousand years from now, we have 10 or 20 times the population that we have now?

How are we going to clothe all those people on Mother Earth? How will development affect the family structure?

With more people on earth, we might need more horses and camels for transportation," said the Anointed One. "More trees will need to be cut down in order to create roadways, which will have a negative environmental impact.

Now, each one of you can understand that by wanting to live longer and healthier, we are increasing the demand that would be placed on Mother Earth for our survival. This could contribute to a potential catastrophe for future generations.

This is a clear example of cause and effect playing out before our vision of the future."

"When you become Sages, not only must you think about the wellbeing of today's generation, you must also understand how present decisions are going to affect future generations.

You have a moral responsibility to leave this world in a better state than how you found it."

While sharing with you my vision of the future, I asked myself this question. "If future generations are going to be so occupied dealing with daily survival issues, do you think that they might not have the time to develop The Sage Within?

Are we going to be the last generation who embrace nature and respects the Laws (codes) of the Cosmic Mind?

Does it worry you to even contemplate that there is a possibility that future generations might not be privileged to the knowledge and understanding that we now have about the various medicinal plants and the benefits of becoming vegetarians?

I do not even want to think of the fact that future generations might not have the knowledge of our Mysticmorphosist!

With more people on earth, do you think that future generations will create more religions? If they do, can they all co-exist or do you think that there are going to be religious wars?

We ancient Mystics and Sages are the present keepers of many of the Secrets of life that are about to be lost, if my vision of the future is true.

Let me share with you why I think future generations are not going to keep this tradition of ours based on this story."

"When I was twelve years old, I was told that when the Creator wanted to hide the secret code of life, he planned to put it on top of the highest mountain or to the bottom of the deepest sea.

Then he said, one day humans will get to the top of the highest mountain and to the bottom of the deepest sea, then, they will easily find the Secret Code of Life.

Then, the Creator decided to hide The Secret Code of Life inside of each human being and he gave each one a pair of eyes that look outward.

Only those who are able to turn their eyes internally will see and behold the manifestation of the Creator Laws of Life."

The Anointed One said; "I sense that future generations will be so occupied looking externally for food, living environment, clothing, and for other daily needs, they will not find quiet moments to turn their eyes internally to find The Secret Code of Life and the manifestation of the Creator in all its glory.

Would future generations continue to fight for the equality of women or build on what we have accomplished, or would they revert to an all-male controlled world?

I hope that each one of you are not just hearing what I am saying, but are listening to every word. It is going to be your responsibility to have answers for those in your villages, who will be asking many of the questions I raised today."

The Anointed One told the group, "I recall while in the Jungle for three months studying the animal kingdom that many on my team, if they were not careful, would have gotten bitten or contracted diseases, which did not affect animals in the jungle."

100

"With the expansion of humans more into what was once the animal kingdom, are we putting ourselves in a position to be more vulnerable to diseases

If there is any truth to that statement, then, the big question we all have to ask is where are future generations going to house all those sick humans? What would happen to our teaching of living in harmony with nature?

Well, I will be leaving this group with a positive attitude because, since we know all the negative effects that our actions can produce, that will affect present and future generations, we are empowered with information that we can use to guide our present actions that will benefit future generations.

Many of you might ask, how I, a single person can, change the world and my answer to you is based on this true story I witnessed in a temple. Everyone was given a candle just before sunset. Hours later, all the candles in the temple were out and the place were in total darkness.

The speaker had a lit candle and used that to light all the other candles and the entire room was as bright as daylight.

If everyone just does his or her part and lights his or her own little candle, said the speaker, collectively, the effect will be amazing. Don't worry about the effect of your single effort, just do your part and all people will have a wonderful and enjoyable life on earth.

In the audience there was a beautiful African Princess by the name of Sharon who wanted to share her Sage Within words of wisdom. She said that it was inspired by The Anointed One with whom she has a great spiritual friendship."

The Anointed One invited Princess Sharon to share those motivated words with everyone.

Princess Sharon walked to the front of the group and these are the words that she spoke:

"I am the Sacred Feminine that was silenced by those who wanted to ascend to my throne, to brush me aside into obscurity in the ash heaps of eternity. However, like Isis & Osiris, I gathered my consciousness, parts and reconnected to my greatness.

I am the Sacred Feminine, the Mother of Creation, the Mother Goddess; I am that I AM, Goddess Eternal. I and my sister Mother Earth are one, we have ascended to the Throne of our being to love, forgive, honor, respect and teach our mystical truths as the Sage Within, never to be silenced in this generation. We will reveal the feminine nature in males and females awakening the Ying and Yang in every being and their connectedness to the universe.

We will use nature's electromagnetic force, the energetic field to reconnect to humanity and all beings. We are ready to express our magical arts to speak, think and move at the speed of light, that's right, my sisters! We are entering into a special time, vibrating at the speed of light and love. We are Love, we are Peace; we are the womb of creation.

Princess Sharon asked the women in the audience to repeat after her these words: "I AM Love, I AM Peace, I AM the Womb of Creation, I AM, I AM, I AM, I AM. Connecting with my Goddess Self I ascend to the divine throne, assuming my rightful place in eternity. Never will I be looked down on, stamped down, thrown out of churches, bibles, sacred texts, dishonored, and placed behind men, hidden from myself and other female goddesses. Those who seek and have sought to hide me are being removed, uprooted and silenced. Yes, Earth Mother is hurtling through space faster than ever in her history to arrive at this moment when earth's axis is tilted back to the time when the Sacred Feminine was honored, worshipped and elevated."

Princess Sharon continued by telling the group that, "We the womb, the incubator, the tree of life that cannot be replaced. Cut the umbilical cord, yes, you are on your own, but Mother Earth still looks after you. Connect with her, ground yourself in her, honor and love her as you love yourself. You will become balanced, whole and spiritually grounded.

You arrive at this sacred space when you can say: I AM a reflection of Mother Earth, I AM the Sacred Feminine, I AM a goddess born into creation each moment, ever manifesting in the now. And so it is."

While thanking Princess Sharon for such profound and captivating words, The Anointed One noticed that everyone's head looked away from her. When she turned her head in their direction, she saw a group of elders walking towards them.

She was flabbergasted when she noticed among the Mystic Elders, the 195 year old Mystic Madiba. Everyone was whispering his name. "That is the *African Mystic Madiba!*"

Mystic Madiba sat next to The Anointed One and said; "I could not miss this great gathering of world Mystics and future Sages."

I sit here before you not as a Mystic, but as a humble servant of you, the people.

In my 195 years traveling this planet, I have met human beings from all walks of life.

You too, one day will meet people of diverse cultures, colors, religions and social ideology.

Many will support your way of life and others might want to persecute you for those same beliefs.

A true seasoned Sage will incorporate *Forgiveness* as part of his or her way of life

Courageous people do not fear forgiving, for the sake of peace," highlighted Mystic Madiba.

Once you adopt the world as your family, you might find yourself not giving quality time to your own family, children and friends. You might be accused of turning your back on those close to you. A true Sage will always be concerned about the wellbeing of humankind, instead of a chosen few.

When you meet people of various shades of color, it is due to the amount of melanin in that person's body. It is therefore a wise thing not to judge a person based on the amount of melanin that person has" said Mystic Madiba to the attentive listeners.

It is important to also know that even though your skin is your largest organ, it is only a fraction of a millimeter thick. Only a wise person will conclude that it makes no sense whatsoever to judge a person's character or social status based on an individual's skin color, which is only a fraction of a millimeter thick.

Based on the above facts, you must reject racial discrimination whether it comes from an African, Indian, Chinese or a European.

No one is born hating another person because of that person's skin color, social background, or religious choices. People learn to hate, and if they can learn to hate, they can be taught to love, for love comes more naturally to the human heart than it's opposite."

Mystic Madiba seemed to have hypnotized the entire group, including The Anointed One. They were all listening attentively to every word he spoke.

Madiba continued his prophetic words by saying: "Since you are not able to create a human being out of nothing, then, you do not have the right to take the life of another. Accept diversity, objections and total rejection without reverting to killing or depriving anyone of their freedom.

If one day you are privileged to be the Chief Elder of your village, you must exercise that position with dignity by making sure that you serve the entire village and not just a chosen few.

It is better to lead from behind and to put others in front, especially when you celebrate victory when nice things occur. You take the front line when there is danger. Then people will appreciate your leadership.

Mystic Madiba closed his presentation by saying:

"I have walked that long road to freedom. I have tried not to falter; I have made missteps along the way. But I have discovered the secret that after climbing a great hill, one only finds that there are many more hills to climb. I have taken a moment here to rest, to steal a view of the glorious vista that surrounds me, to look back on the distance I have come."

"But I can only rest for a moment, for with freedom come responsibilities, and I dare not linger, for my long walk is not ended."

The Anointed One thanked the great Mystic Madiba for his special appearance and words of wisdom. She then turned to the group and said:

"Pack your bags, and let us begin this journey by awakening The Sage Within and become great stewards of Mother Earth for the betterment of all humankind!

"Let us follow Mystic Madiba's footsteps by finding the path to our Mental, Physical and Spiritual Freedom.

Have a safe journey on becoming a Sage and remember these words: *Never try to become an adult. Adults are the most miserable people on earth. They are too old to do too many things. Remain a responsible child, regardless how old you are…Die Young at an Old Age..."*

www.ingramcontent.com/pod-product-compliance
Lightning Source LLC
LaVergne TN
LVHW021537080426
835509LV00019B/2691